JESUS THE JEW

WHAT DOES IT MEAN THAT JESUS IS A JEW ?

JESUS THE JEW

ISRAEL AND THE PALESTINIANS

•

MARKUS BARTH

Translated by Frederick Prussner

•

JOHN KNOX PRESS
ATLANTA

232
.685
B 284 j E

Library of Congress Cataloging in Publication Data

Barth, Markus.
  Jesus the Jew.

  Translation of Der Jude Jesus, Israel und die
Palästinenser.
    1. Jesus Christ—Relation to Judaism—Addresses,
essays, lectures. 2. Jewish-Arab relations—
Addresses, essays, lectures. I. Title.
BT590.J8B3713   261.2   77-15741
ISBN 0-8042-0834-4

FOREWORD

This book contains two lectures originally delivered in 1973/74 to assemblies devoted to the cooperation of Jews and Christians. In making the revision necessary for publication, the original purpose was adhered to, namely, to address those Jews and Christians and indeed all persons of goodwill who are looking for a new or deepened understanding of Israel and of the church, especially in respect to their service to truth and justice, to freedom and peace. Further amendments made for the American edition include the rewriting of large sections in the light of external and internal developments during the last few years.

The intention of both parts of this book is to point out the unbreakable ties, even the solidarity, between the church and Israel. My thesis is: for Christians there is no loyalty to Jesus, the great brother of all humans, without a critical solidarity with all the Jewish brothers and sisters who are living today, particularly with the Israelis who are fighting for survival. There is, however, also for the Israelis no other way to survival —and for Christians no other way to support them—than by reflecting anew about faith and loyalty and by a new structuring of the relationship to the Palestinians. What is at stake is nothing less than the relationship between faith and life or between the love of God and the love for the neighbor. Of course, there is no attempt to reach a general decision regarding the sense or nonsense of catchwords such as "political" or "politicized theology." Much more we hope to show that faith in God calls for the assumption of social and political responsibilities, for negating the false sense of security, and for an engagement in word and deed which offers support to the Jewish people in their struggle and their mission among the nations.

For this purpose we have presented information that stems

from the Bible, other books, daily news, and also personal encounters. The intention is to discuss priorities, fight against
ignorance and prejudices, and keep up the hope for peace.

The combination of biblical observations with a call to
repentance and engagement has so far been received with
widely different reactions. While the speech "What Does It
Mean That Jesus Is a Jew?" met with approval, the discussion
of the relationship between "Israel and the Palestinians" provoked passionate protest among a part of the listeners. Many
found it incomprehensible that the same author could apparently contradict himself so blatantly. They viewed the second
lecture as a slander of the first. Instead of New Testament
theological proclamation they considered it a one-sided political agitation in favor of the New Left. The well-founded yes to
Israel seemed in a scandalous way to have been replaced by a
subsequent rude no.

Individual readers as well as study groups in congregations
are invited to ponder whether such a contradiction really exists. The brotherhood between Jews and Christians proves true
only when both sides do not dodge the pain of *critical* solidarity.

Markus Barth
Basel, April 1978

CONTENTS

What Does It Mean That Jesus Is a Jew?
9

Israel and the Palestinians
41

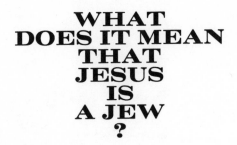

**WHAT
DOES IT MEAN
THAT
JESUS
IS
A JEW
?**

WHAT DOES IT MEAN THAT JESUS IS A JEW?

Many people today apparently find it possible to separate the memory of the *Jew* Jesus from the belief in Jesus Christ. To state that Jesus is a Jew is to insult, distress, annoy, and, indeed, provoke them to the point of contradiction, suspicion, and hatred. I want to describe, first of all, how and from whom in recent years I have experienced that kind of opposition—especially in conversations and at conferences.

I. Protests

A. Christian and non-Christian Arabs sometimes hear in this statement the claim that Jesus was an Israeli. Thus, they suspect that this claim is held chiefly by those people who would like to give legitimacy and support to the Zionists. Zionists, however, according to one Arab understanding of this concept, are those people who, with the help of Western politics, Western armaments, and Western capital, have pushed into the realm of Arab culture and sovereignty and have turned millions of people into second-class citizens, into oppressed inhabitants of occupied territories, and into miserable refugees or desperate fanatics. Even when Western Christians, in using the statement about Jesus, want only to declare that the hope of the Christians is the same as that of the Jews (see Acts 23:6; 26:6; 28:20), this is regarded as intolerable. As early as 1954 at the conference of the World Council of Churches in Evanston, such a declaration was branded by Christian speakers from the Near East as an attempt to bestow a biblical sanction upon the State of Israel.

Arab scholars—including Christians as well as Moslems—frequently draw from the history of ideas or of religion to protest any reflection on the Jewish origin and character of Jesus. Moslem scholars speak of a three-stage development of monotheism, one which progresses from Judaism by way of Christianity to Islam. Similarly, their Christian colleagues, such as the German philosopher G. F. W. Hegel, emphasize only the irreversible progressive development from Judaism to Christianity. There are thus Moslems and Christians who seem to agree that particularism which focuses only on one stage or culture is now over. A worldwide, more comprehensive universalism is taking its place. There has been an advance from a religion which is tied to locality and land to the worship of God in spirit and in truth (see John 4:23–24). In distinction, however, anyone who says that Jesus is a Jew is trying—so it is argued—to turn back the wheel of history.

What is the origin of this relative harmony between Christian and Moslem Arabs with which they confront Jewish and Christian Zionism? One of the reasons for this agreement (which for us Westerners is so surprising) certainly is the continuing hard struggle of the Arab Christians for survival in their Moslem surroundings. And it is no wonder that non-Arab Christians in Asia and Africa who are aware of this struggle also support the attitude of the Arabs and make it their own.

B. The statement that Jesus is a Jew also, however, seems to evoke distress among certain *Jews*. It is true that Jewish scholars like Rosenzweig, Baeck, Montefiore, Klausner, Buber, Flusser, and Ben Chorin have, in contrast to Hegel's philosophy of religion and of history, contributed abundantly and decisively to the renewed recognition of the genuinely Jewish substance and intention of the life and teaching of Jesus. In doing this they unmask the presumptuous claims which Christians have made for originality and superiority over the Jews.

But even when Christians recognize how much they all, including Jesus himself, owe to Judaism, they still have not overcome the problem. Jews continue to have sufficient cause for resentment. By itself the acknowledgment that Jesus is a Jew does not at all mean that the historic anti-Semitism of the church is thereby really regretted, retracted, and buried. This painful issue is illustrated by four examples taken from important experiences of Jewish-Christian encounter and dialogue.

Each suggests that while the readiness for understanding is great a genuine reconciliation is still far off.

1. *The Declaration of the Second Vatican Council Concerning the Jews* (Nostra aetate, chap. IV) was completed in 1965 with the forceful assistance of Abraham Heschel from New York. In summary it stated that Christians are or should be grateful for the Jewish legacy on which they are still feeding. The conclusion drawn from this was that the Jews ought no longer to be regarded collectively as "god-killing" and "perfidious" fellow human beings who were responsible for the crucifixion of Jesus and the role of Judas Ischariot. The Council acknowledged that Jesus Christ and all that the Christians owe to him was first promised and given to the Jews, and that even after Christ's death the Jews remain most dear to God. But— and this is the reason why Abraham Heschel himself could not be satisfied with what had been achieved—one must ask whether the claim to a Christian monopoly in the administration of the legacy has really been relinquished. Indeed, it was implicitly acknowledged that great spiritual riches which originally had belonged to the Jews were inherited, borrowed, or taken over by the Christians. But this acknowledgment does not exclude the notion that the Church is the sole legitimate heir and has the right to behave accordingly. The Second Vatican Council classifies Judaism among the "non-Christian religions."

2. An example from the Reformation churches dates from an earlier time. In 1523 Luther published a work entitled, *That Jesus Christ Was Born a Jew*. Though this title may lead us to expect an answer to the question with which we are concerned we in fact discover that only surprise and disappointment are in store. We are told that Jesus Christ was prophesied in the Old Testament precisely as the one who at Augustus' time actually appeared, and that the Jews ought promptly and completely to convert to Jesus Christ. That is to say they should let themselves be baptized, because now, thanks to the Reformation, the gospel was again being preached in its pure and genuine form. Luther's hope was not fulfilled. For this reason he

wrote twenty years later two abominable pamphlets, *On the Jews and Their Lies* and *The Shem Hamphoras and the Lineage of Christ*. No wonder that to Jewish ears the statement, that Jesus was a Jew, can still sound as though a new imperialistic call for total surrender is thereby extended, namely, the demand for an immediate conversion to Christianity. Among other well-founded anxieties, this particular one is outstanding.

3. In the New Testament and during the course of the history of the church, Isaiah 53, the chapter about the suffering servant of God, has been understood as a prophecy pointing to Jesus Christ. The wording and the original sense of the chapter within its context can, however, also be understood as a statement about the whole people of God (or its "remnant"), rather than about an individual person. While these two views are not necessarily incompatible, the church's interpretation might possess more credibility for Jews if the confession of faith in the suffering Jesus Christ were combined with a willingness on our part to suffer more unselfishly for the sake of Jesus Christ. This was the position taken, for instance, by the evangelists Matthew and Luke, the apostles Peter and Paul, and the seer John. The christological interpretation of Isaiah 53, however, is discredited when people calling themselves Christians combine their reliance upon Jesus Christ's unique suffering with the judgment that all Jews of the past and present are guilty of Jesus' death. In doing this, Christians have shouldered an enormous burden of guilt. Either as spectators or as secret promoters of pagan anti-Semitism, they consent and/or contribute to the defamation, persecution, and murder of Jews—while they themselves look for security and power. A Jew once said to me: "You leave suffering to the Jewish people and love us Jews only as long as we are like the lamb that is innocently slaughtered. But if we succeed, as we did in the Six-Day War, in stepping forth as the Lion of Judah, you take away your sympathy from us and leave us alone while you quote Isaiah 53 and seek quiet and security for yourselves by all means possible." The famous statues on the Strassburg cathedral do indeed illustrate how

readily the synagogue has been seen as the figure of suffering and the church, on the other hand, as the triumphant mistress. The confession of faith in Jesus, the crucified Jew, affects many Jews like a smirking grimace: the Jews are allowed to pay the price for this confession.

4. There are Christians who take these Jewish grievances to heart. In disposition and behavior, in word and deed, they really want to do penance for the subtle as well as crude forms of anti-Semitism (more accurately, anti-Judaism). By witnessing to their solidarity with the Jews and to their love for the Jews, they want to make this contrition effective and visible. Jewish-Christian dialogues take place at many levels: biblical, historical, cultural, and liturgical; and in many places: study groups, private homes, business, and chance meetings. Periodicals for general information and scholarly exchange have been founded; mutual support and joint undertakings take place; friendships have been established and some mutual understanding is growing. Nevertheless an abominable prejudice can continue to be at work as is shown by the following example. A Jew once asked me why I was especially interested in the Jews, why I was participating in the dialogue, and why I was standing up for justice—even for the State of Israel. Led by a desire to recognize the injustice tolerated or done by us, I answered that I loved this people for the sake of Christ. In accord with the theme of these pages, I might have answered, ". . . because Jesus is a Jew." At any rate, my partner in this conversation replied, "Thanks, but I can do without such a love for somebody else's sake. That is not at all a love for me or for other Jews but a love which uses me only as a trigger, as a means to an end, or as a transparent foil. You Christians thus have actually, on the basis of your reading of the Old Testament and of your bad conscience towards us, created an image of what a Jew is or should be. You do not ask about our own self-understanding, our better or worse features, but you subsist on your conception of the Jewish mission among the nations [the Dutch document *Israel, People, Land, and State,* 1971, could have been named as an example] and are in love with the image you

make for yourselves of us. You do not, however, really take part in the pride and despair, victories and defeats of individual Jews and of the State of Israel." The reaction of this Jew shows that my answer to his question—all noble intentions notwithstanding—was not good. If I had spoken of Auschwitz and of the co-responsibility of Christian theologians and church attitudes in that event, most likely he would have been equally unhappy: then I would have loved him for the murdered Jews' sake. Perhaps his question was unfair; at any rate, I still do not know how I should have answered it. Years ago a black American colleague remarked that we white liberals and friends of integration tried to prove our friendship for the blacks by never contradicting them seriously, never speaking our minds when we were mad at them, but always attempting only to "understand" them and letting them have their own way. He saw in this attitude (and rightly so!) an abysmal contempt and inhumanity. For among brothers and sisters one can, may, and must contradict one another vigorously and speak one's mind.

C. But what does the statement, Jesus is a Jew, mean for *Christians?*

1. We certainly do not need to pay any attention to those Christians *(Deutsche Christen)* who during the period of Adolf Hitler's regime (1933–1945) wanted to provide Jesus with a certificate of Aryan descent. Far more serious is the objection to Jesus' Jewishness which—with or without an appeal to a passage in Paul's Second Letter to the Corinthians—rests on a complete lack of interest in the historical origins, dates, and facts, in short, in the *curriculum vitae* and the earthly ministry of Jesus of Nazareth. Indeed, in 2 Corinthians 5:16 the apostle Paul belittles a regard for Christ "from the human point of view," and according to some German interpreters of the Bible this means that all elements of Jesus' "earthly life" are immaterial for faith. However, Pauline polemics are not directed against Jesus Christ's history between his conception and his death, but rather against a "fleshly kind" of understanding the Christ. These polemics, in the context of the problems raised in Corinth, protest the attempt to transform the wisdom of God

revealed in Christ into a theosophy. A false spiritualization of Jesus is called a fleshly enterprise! A modern counterpart of this lack of concern for the appearance of God's Son in human history and life is found wherever the Jewish origin (nationality) and nature of Jesus are artificially separated from the Christ who is confessed by the churches. For instance, in the *Systematic Theology* of Paul Tillich (Chicago: University of Chicago Press, I, 1951, pp. 133–35; II, 1957, p. 123) the crucifixion means that Jesus sacrifices himself as a specific historical figure—including all that is both symbolical and tied to place and time—in favor of the timeless and universal significance of Christ. "The Christ" is now to be understood as the transcending principle of participation in the Ground of Being. Already the 18th century German philosopher and poet, G. E. Lessing, had argued that a fortuitous historical truth cannot constitute the basis of an eternal rational truth. For Tillich, certainly the absolutizing of a symbol constitutes the essence of the religious Fall. Thus, there are Christians who *de facto* agree with the Arab and Hegelian point of view mentioned earlier: ironically they turn back the wheel of history in inadmissable ways when the Jewishness of Jesus is given special emphasis.

2. Another protest, allegedly objective and scientific and yet perhaps unconscious, against Jesus the Jew is found in many commentaries on the Gospel of Matthew, especially in the comments made on chapter 5:17–20. Words are transmitted in this passage which express an unfailingly positive attitude on the part of Jesus towards the Mosaic Law. Many commentaries and monographs, however, declare the words about "not abolishing but fulfilling" and about the permanent validity of the law to be inauthentic. They ascribe to the "historical Jesus" nothing more than a "radicalization of the Law" and understand this radicalization at most as preparing the way for Paul's preaching which is alleged to proclaim "the end of the law." They absolve the historical Jesus from any loyalty to the spirit and the letter of the Law—and, thereby, to Judaism. To be a Jew means, of course, to be bound by and to the Law—whether it be in orthodox, conservative, or reform ways or even

in the protest against the Law which cannot get away from its object. Even Paul did not want to "overthrow but to uphold" the law by his preaching of Christ (Rom. 3:31). Wherever learned pens describe Jesus as an alternative to the will of God which was revealed in the Law of Moses and in the prophetic interpretation of the Law, and wherever the proclamation contained in the allegedly pre-gospel document Q with its fundamental yes to the Law is described as half- or sub-Christian, the statement that Jesus is a Jew is called into question. Then the significance of his relation to the Law and the people of the Jews is reduced and misunderstood.

3. Finally, there are Christians who feel painfully affected by the statement that Jesus is a Jew: it reminds them of what happened in Auschwitz, Maidenek, and Treblinka. They realize that, together with the millions of Jews who were murdered there, Jesus Christ also was once again crucified at the hands of baptized people. They deem it psychologically unhealthy to be reminded all too frequently and all too strongly of the crime committed both on Good Friday and during the pogroms against the Jews of earlier and more recent date. They would rather turn to contemporary problems such as assistance to developing nations, justice for oppressed people and minorities, public health care and the promotion of personality development, than to a re-examination and redress of unsolved problems inherited from almost two thousand years of church history.

In summary, because of the existing loud or silent protests from Arab, Jewish, and Christian quarters, "Jesus the Jew" appears to be an undesirable, in any case, a very ambiguous phenomenon which has little to do with faith. For this reason, to emphasize his Jewishness seems to be decidedly inopportune, perhaps also irrelevant, and finally politically, theologically, and psychologically harmful.

All of this cannot get around the fact that references in the New Testament to the Jewish origin, the Jewish nature, indeed also the Jewish history of Jesus are particularly numerous, emphatic, and impressive.

II. The Biblical Testimony

1. Probably very soon after the resurrection, and perhaps first in Jerusalem, Jesus was called "off-spring [seed] of David." (Rom. 1:3) For its confession and proclamation the Christian community appropriated the designation "Son of David" which occasionally had been used already before the death of Jesus (Matt. 9:27; 15:22; 20:30–31; 21:9, 15; 22:41–46). The genealogies of Jesus in Matthew 1 and Luke 3 serve to prove the physical descent of Jesus from the well-known king of Judah. These references to the "Son of David," however, are not merely concerned with physical matters. The mention of Jesus' davidic origin includes a hint at the way he acted and at the extension of his realm. David shook off the yoke of the Philistines, and under his rule the boundaries of Israel reached an extent never to be repeated in Israel's history. It is, however, a mistake to see embodied in the "Son of David" none other than political aspirations and hopes—as though early Christians wanted only to hail Jesus as a new Judas Maccabeus or leader of zealots. In popular piety, nourished as it was by the great number of psalms of lament, penitence, petition, and thanksgiving that mention David's name in the prescript, David is the prototype of the poor man who is chosen by God but is chased around during his entire life (before and after his enthronement), who looks upon himself as a dog who has no way out except to cry to God for help and to rely upon him. The strongest King of the Jews endured the worst fate—and the Lord heard him and saved him out of all his troubles (Ps. 34). Jewish-born contemporaries of Jesus had probably more than genealogical and nationalistic interests in mind when they called him "Son of David." Certainly in these calls personal distress played a far greater role than the duress caused by the Roman occupation. To be a Jew and to appeal to Jesus, the Son of David means, therefore, for those supplicants to be chosen but still to be chastised, to be helpless but still certain of help and of a helper (cf. 2 Sam. 7:14–15).

2. Paul speaks of Jesus, born of a woman and subject to the

Law, as having fulfilled the just demands of the Law (Gal. 4:4;
Rom. 5:19; 8:4; 10:4). The life and death of Jesus Christ embodied the sum of the Law: the love of the neighbor (Gal. 2:20; 5:14;
Rom. 13:8–10; 1 Cor. 13; Eph. 5:2, 25). Because Paul designates
this Jesus Christ as "Abraham's seed" (Rom. 4:13; Gal. 3:16)
and repeatedly speaks—in literal translation—of the "faith of
Christ Jesus" (Gal. 2:16, 20; 3:22,26; Rom. 1:17; 3:22–26; Phil.
3:9) he shows that the Messiah leads and concludes the line of
those who are justified by faith (cf. Heb. 12:1–2). To be a Jew,
accordingly, means to fulfill the promise and the Law through
faith and love. But the concept, "Abraham's seed [or son]," has
a further meaning. Abraham (etymologized as "father of many
nations," Gen. 17:5) already in Paul's day perhaps was considered to be a sort of patron saint for the Gentiles who were
turning to the Jewish faith, the so-called proselytes. If Christ
is a Jew of Abraham's type, then he is a man who does not put
his light under a bushel but lets it shine. True to the mission
of Israel he is a "light to the Gentiles." (Isa. 42:6; 49:6)

3. In the Gospel of John—in agreement with Matthew,
Mark, and Luke—Nazareth is identified as the home of Jesus'
family. Little good was expected from there, least of all the
Messiah as can be seen from the name, "Galilee of the Gentiles," "people which sat in darkness" (Matt. 4:14–16) and from
the derisive remarks, such as, "what good can come out of
Nazareth?" and, "the Messiah surely does not come from Galilee!" (John 1:46; 7:41) Of course, there is no denial that Galilee
belongs to Israel, but its population was suspect of ignoring the
Law. What in the eyes of some Jews made Jesus despicable was
his origin from Galilee, which is recorded by all canonical Gospels as essential. Further, there were priestly circles (in Jerusalem and in Qumran) which could imagine the preservation,
deliverance, and restoration of Israel by no other means save
priestly domination. The Letter to the Hebrews (7:14), however,
which is so interested in the service of the priesthood, empha-
sizes (together with the genealogies in Matthew 1 and Luke 3)
that it "is evident that our Lord was descended from the royal
tribe of Judah." The Jewish origin of Jesus is apparently no

guarantee of his acceptance by all Jews but causes doubts, debates, and contradictory opinions. Jews differ from one another in their understanding of the hallmark or criteria of true Judaism.

4. Jesus himself says a full yes to all Jews: "salvation comes from the Jews." (John 4:22) He says to the poorest among the Jews: "blessed are they who are poor through and through." (Literally, "in spirit," Matt. 5:3.) The disciples are told to go first only to the lost sheep of Israel; the bread is to be given to the children, not to the dogs (Matt. 10:6, 23; 15:24, 26).

However because the same gospels contain a whole succession of conflict scenes between the Jewish guardians of the Law and Jesus, it has been surmised that Jesus, the Jew, had inwardly turned away from the basis, directive, and criterion of Jewish worship, the Law. Indeed, he did interpret the Law forcefully and mercifully at the same time—sometimes in ways similar to the highly respected and influential Rabbi Hillel— and he castigated a hypocritical fulfillment of arbitrarily executed commandments. Yet it seemed as if he also broke it: he sat at the same table with sinners; he permitted eating with unwashed hands; he allowed work on the Sabbath and performed it himself as a healer; he touched lepers and noticeably disrupted the service of sacrifices by cleansing the temple. He was characterized as a blasphemer by the Sadducean high priest with the approval of the Sanhedrin, though without evident cause. The opinion is widespread that his deviation and alienation from Judaism was the presupposition of the religious progress which he brought to humankind. His Jewish origin would in this case at best form the cause of tragic conflict with people of his own kind. To my mind this view is not justified. For change and progress can take place within Judaism. As a matter of fact, they have taken place throughout Judaism —not only despite Judaism. Any Jew, whether a prophet, a Chasid, a wise man, a rabbi, or a Pharisee, will come into conflict with the official guardians of the Law of the day, specifically when making a radical effort to be obedient to the Law in word and deed. Even among the Pharisees with their zeal for the Law there were quarrels between the radical Shammaites and the more humane Hillelites. In turn, the groups of Qumran zealots and charismatic prophets of doomsday had their own notions of obedience to the Law. To this day there is no study of the Law, no question about the application of the Law, no problem of loyalty to God's Law in emergency situations, which does not evoke vigorous disputes among the Jews—one needs only to think about the mobilization of the armed forces of the State of Israel during the Yom Kippur services in October 1973. Precisely because Jesus completely affirmed the Law of God in word and deed, his teaching and behavior inevitably had to give offense to both the pious people and the religious establishment. To be a Jew means to bear up under and to suffer through such conflict and opposition among one's own people. *Jewish* writings contain a tradition which has to do with persecuted and slain prophets.

5. The description of Jesus' belonging to the Jewish people is particularly meaningful in those reports in Matthew and Luke which have to do with the virgin birth. This birth in no way encroaches upon his Jewish origins. Even today a Jew is a person who, according to the statutes of the orthodox rabbinate, has a Jewish mother. The mention of the virgin Mary in the Gentile Christian "Apostolic Creed" thus means that Jesus' Jewish origins are gratefully and admiringly acknowledged. Of course, the exclusion of Joseph also carries with it a crucial affirmation. Why did a virgin become the mother of Jesus?

(a) As their frequent references to the Old Testament and to Jewish traditions and customs show, the authors of Matthew and Luke were Jewish Christians. It is most unlikely that in speaking of the virgin birth they associated with virginity the notion or proof of special purity, more specifically, of a moral qualification for becoming and being the "Mother (of the Son) of God." For according to Jewish understanding, virginity and the condition of being unmarried are a deficiency, not a merit. The notion that chastity is a qualification for particular kinds of service is found, for example, among the Roman vestal virgins, but among the Jews only in heretical fringegroups.

(b) There are indications that in the ancient world the combination of virginity and motherhood was a symbol of a movement for women's liberation, and even of the autarchy of women—as if to say, a ray from the sun, a ball thrown into our lap is enough; we can become pregnant even without you men. The biblical reports about Jesus' birth have just as little to do with such glorifications of the virginal mother as with the rejection of sexual relationships by ascetics.

(c) The Matthean representation of Jesus' birth shows that Mary was ("sociologically") considered to belong among suspect, unfaithful women and that in this perspective Jesus would have grown up as a bastard had Joseph not adopted him as his own child. And Luke makes clear that Israel's visitation through the gift of the Messiah is equivalent to a new creation and not just a display of a power which Israel herself possessed. It is, therefore, not a "pure" remnant of Israel, represented by a sinless Mary, which gives to the world its redeemer but the intervention of God the Creator. That the Messiah is born in and from Israel is not an honor for which Israel can take credit; rather it is sheer grace. He is a Jew who dares to acknowledge that human beings live only by such grace. By virtue of this grace it also happens that women like Elizabeth, this or that Mary, the prophetess Anna, the Samaritan woman at Jacob's well, Phoebe, Lois, Priscilla, and others are given a voice and become, along with chosen men, fully qualified witnesses for Jesus Christ.

6. Few specific details are provided by the New Testament about the manner of Jesus' Second Coming. The ascension of Jesus which, according to Acts 1:9–12, took place on the Mount of Olives, is interpreted as an anticipation of his return: "He will come in the same way as you saw him go into heaven." This is not the place to decide whether this means, as a medieval tradition claims (based on Zech. 14:4 and Rom. 11:26?) that the return will be localized on the Mount of Olives. What matters is that he who became human will return in human form for the validation, perfection, and glorification of all he suffered, did, and said. Just as he was a Jew he will be a Jew again—

otherwise he would deny his humanity and the history of salvation which is linked to Israel. God's faithfulness to Israel is revealed and assured by the Messiah's origin "according to the flesh" from Israel and by the salvation of all Israel through his coming (Rom. 9:5; 11:25–26).

III. Emphases in the Biblical Testimony

1. The New Testament declarations which explicitly point to the Jewishness of Jesus are supported and strengthened by a remarkable fact. Almost on every page of the New Testament we find either quotations or concepts, thought forms, and lines of thought taken from the Old Testament. Numerous also are the general references which point to Jesus' mission, coming, work, suffering, death, resurrection, and rule as having occurred "according to the scriptures." (Rom. 1:2; 3:21; 1 Cor. 15:3–4; John 5:46; 12:13–15; Heb. 1:1ff.; Luke 1:46–55, 68–79; 2:29–32; 7:22–27; 24:26–27, 44–45; Acts 2:16–21, 25–31, 34–35; Matt. *passim,* etc.) The titles by which Jesus is named and the vocabulary chosen to describe his work (e.g., in Luke 4:17–19; Matt. 3:17; 11:2–10; 16:16; 21:4–5, 9; 26:64) make the Old Testament influence clear: even Gentiles are dependent on the connection between Israel's hope and Jesus of Nazareth when they wish to confess that Jesus is the Christ (Luke 2:30–32). Frequently New Testament descriptions of the church, be they affirmative or critical, are made in the form of quotations of Old Testament promises or calls to repentance extended to God's people. In both Testaments a similar faith and confession, hardening and denial are found. Abraham believed the promise and was justified by grace (Rom. 4; Gal. 3). Love of God and the neighbor is the sum of the commandments (Luke 10:27–28; James 2:8; Rom. 13:8–10). There is no divine wisdom except that which is embodied in the crucified Jesus Christ (1 Cor. 1—2; Matt. 11:16–19, 25–30). The stone which the builders have rejected is made the cornerstone of the temple built by God out of human beings (1 Pet. 2:4–10).

Old Testament elements are not endorsed only because of their value as timeless symbols which can be arbitrarily appropriated or transformed. For the specific hopes of specific persons and the meaning of unique, namely Jewish, words and institutions are pointed out when the Old Testament resounds in the New. It is also not a question of an apologetic "proof from prophecy"—as though the authors of the New Testament writings either had wanted to adorn their faith with the patina of antiquity or had considered the truth of their declarations as being proved by the correspondence between prediction and fulfillment. They were wise enough to know that much that is old is hopelessly antiquated (Matt. 5:21–48; 9:17; Gal. 3:19—4:7; Heb. 8:13) and that a mere correspondence between oracle and event does not by any means prove that the person in whom predictions are fulfilled is God's Son. They did, however, understand Jesus Christ, as well as the faith, the love, the community of believers made up of both Jews and Gentiles, to be the continuation and coronation of God's history with Israel. They wanted this history to serve as the only hermeneutical key to an understanding of the events surrounding Jesus. And they made it clear that worship and service of God can only then take place "in spirit and in truth" (John 4:24) when in both affirmative and critical ways it takes up and perfects the worship of Israel. The Letter to the Hebrews shows this with particular clarity.

For this reason the Old Testament is not cited in the New as authenticating literature but as an invitation to listen to the dialogue between God and Israel and to join in it. Paul, for example, is persuaded (2 Cor. 1:20) that in Jesus Christ there is contained the sum of the divine promise (God's yes-word) and of the human response (the amen).

2. The New Testament stresses emphatically that there is only *one* person, *one* descendant of Abraham, *one* son of David, *one* priest, *one* prophet, *one* mediator, *one* Son of God, and *one* wise man who is judge over all Jews and Gentiles. His name is Jesus. The sound of rejoicing which is characteristic of this announcement—it is made in the form of simple confessions, elaborate hymns, or drawn-out arguments—does include the rejection of other beliefs. Often, particularly in John's Gospel,

in the book of Acts, and in the Letters of Paul, there is a polemic which is directed against the Jews. For this reason the question arises whether the New Testament is not, in the final analysis, a renunciation of Judaism.

John's Gospel does not compel one to answer affirmatively. For there are passages which speak of the Jews in a positive sense: "an Israelite without guile" (1:47); "salvation comes from the Jews" (4:22); "many of the Jews . . . believed in him" (7:31; 8:31; 11:45); Nicodemus is a leading Jew (3:1), and Jesus is crucified as "King of the Jews" (18:33, 37, 39; 19:3, 19, etc.). If "the Jews" are characterized as children of the devil, of a murderer, and of a liar (8:44), that is because among the Jews there are such who do not believe in Jesus (7:48) but instead persecute him and want to kill him (5:16, 18; 7:1; 10:31, etc.). It is certain that the writer of the Gospel, in several of these polemical passages, had in mind the ruling Sadducean majority in the high council, in others simply "the Judaeans," namely, the inhabitants of the former Southern kingdom of Judah. Galileans and Samaritans, each group in its own way, had been treated with contempt by the Judaeans long before Jesus' coming; this resulted in counterattacks of the Galileans and Samaritans. When finally in the book of Acts the blame for the death of Jesus and the persecution of the early Christian community is charged to the Jewish authorities, even this does not mean an abandonment of the promise given to Israel. Stephen's speech in particular (Acts 7) makes it clear that the appearance of Jesus and of the Christian community brought *internal* Jewish controversies to their climax. Accordingly, the debate over the law of the Jews in particular, as reflected in Paul's Letters, is interpreted also by Jewish specialists in Pauline studies, such as H. J. Schoeps and Shalom Ben Chorin, as an internal Jewish, not an anti-Jewish polemic. According to W. D. Davies' revolutionary book, *Paul and Rabbinic Judaism* (London: S.P.C.K., 1948), it is Paul who is a typical Jewish Christian.

The connection of Jesus with Judaism is, therefore, neither denied nor diminished in the New Testament, nor is it overshadowed by an alternative. But it is made clear that Jesus was no more than *one* Jew, and that the concept, "the Jew," actually should not exist at all. One cannot define "the Jew" or "the Jews"—neither as a nation nor as a religion, nor as a creed, nor as a culture. It is possible to speak, however, of a people which derives its name (etymologically) from a vocation or desire "to praise God." (Gen. 29:35; cf. Rom. 2:17–29) In spite of all murmuring and rebellion in their ranks, this people cannot free themselves from God because God does not dismiss them, whatever they might do or suffer. The special relation of God to Israel continues without interruption, even after the crucifixion of Jesus and the beginning of the successful mission to the Gentiles (Rom. 9—11). If ever there was a break, it was only in the Godforsakenness of Jesus at the cross.

In any case, according to the New Testament the Jewish origin, the Jewish nature, and the Jewish life of Jesus signify that this man made his appearance as a member of a people which was torn to pieces by inner conflicts. The priestly (Sadducean) circles which ruled in Jerusalem; their pietistic yet also on occasion politically very active Pharisaic adversaries; the Zealots who were inclined toward fanatical and terroristic action; the despised Samaritans; the self-confident community of Qumran (not mentioned in the New Testament except perhaps indirectly in Acts 6:7, in polemical allusions in the Sermon on the Mount, in Luke 1—2, and in Pauline formulations concerning the gracious righteousness of God); also baptist movements like that of John in the Jordan Valley; cultural assimilators from the diaspora like Philo; but also fanatics for the Law from the dispersion and critics of the temple (from the diaspora or the earlier Northern Kingdom? cf. Stephen)—all stood in opposition to each other and passed sentences of mutual damnation on one another. They were all Jews. Jesus with his little band of disciples and women constituted only *one* phenomenon of truly Jewish existence.

Such an existence is not a secure possession or condition in which, in all tranquility, one can comfortably take delight. It does not solve à problem but creates it. At any point in history,

a Jew lives in tension with other Jews. Continually he or she
has to make decisions which may disrupt the harmony and
communion with other Jews. Such a life is marked by continu-
ous trials of faith and by great suffering at the hands of one's
own people. Jesus experienced this pain: "Now the judgment is
come over this world"; "the judgment consists in this: that the
light came into the world and that people loved the darkness
more than the light"; "his own people did not receive him";
"again a division arose among the Jews." (John 12:31; 3:19;
1:11; 10:19) Jesus weeps and laments over Jerusalem because
this city has not recognized what will make for its peace but,
instead, continues the murder of prophets and therefore will
eventually be left in ruins (Luke 19:41-44; Matt. 23:27—24:2).
Such an announcement of judgment upon Israel and such
weeping over the chosen people has been ever since the days of
Moses and of Jeremiah not a sign of an anti-Jewish attitude but
of a genuine love for Israel. Only a false prophet announces
"peace, peace," where there really is no peace. Radical conversion ("repentance") is again and again requested of this people
—no less than of the Christian congregations, e.g., Revelation
2—3.

3. Everything that is said in the New Testament regarding
the crisis which was called forth by Jesus among the Jewish
people is described as relevant not only for the Jews but also
for all other human beings. Repeatedly the Gospel of John calls
the Judaeans "the world" and identifies "the world" with the
Judaeans. This does not mean that all Jews are considered
particularly malignant, but rather that they represent the
whole world. What is said in Matthew's Gospel against the
Pharisees is also directed (maybe even primarily) against certain circles of the Christian community (in Antioch?) which
consisted of both Jews and Gentiles. In the ninth chapter of the
Letter to the Romans, the two sons of Rebecca, Jacob and Esau,
represent Israel and the Gentiles. Similarly, according to Galatians 4:21-31, the two sons of Abraham, Isaac and Ishmael,
stand for the Church which includes Gentile Christians, and for
the "present Jerusalem" respectively. According to the Letter

to the Ephesians (2:13–17) the temporary conflict between the Jews who had remained home and those who had been exiled and their reunification in peace under *one* shepherd represent nothing else than the tension between and the reconciliation of *Jews* and *Gentiles*. Even today in a number of Jewish Passover liturgies, but also in the songs and sermons of black communities in the U.S.A. and in all theology which is socially and ethically oriented, the liberation which was bestowed upon the people of Israel in the Exodus is celebrated as the prototype of the liberation of *all* oppressed and exploited people.

From this one must conclude that the New Testament remains true to Israel when—with very different emphases in its various parts which cannot individually be given their due here—it regards the Jews as the pioneer and representative people for all peoples. Their hardness of heart has a parallel in the hardness of heart of the Gentiles, as is shown by a comparison between Matthew 13:14–15, Romans 9:17–18; 11:8, 10; Ephesians 4:18 and Acts 28:14–28. Old Testament statements which describe Israel's apostasy into idolatry are used in Romans 1:18–23 in the description of pagan worship. According to the apostle Paul, the need of salvation by sheer grace is equally total among Jews and Gentiles. For "there is no difference": the Jews have sinned *against* the Law, and the Gentiles have sinned even *without* (having) the Law. Both are found guilty before God and have no way to be saved except to rely solely on a deliverance through grace (Rom. 2:12; 3:22–31; Gal. 2: 15–21). Israel, to be sure, is a special case in God's historical dealings with human beings. Israel's special character, however, consists in the fact that this people in its ups and downs, its splits and hopes for unity, its dispersals and gatherings, its disobedience and its efforts at obedience is representative of God's will towards *all* people.

Nevertheless, the Jews are not only types or models of this will—they are also God's instruments. That is true not only of Abraham, Jonah, and Saul/Paul, but especially of the Jew Jesus. Israel's mission to the Gentiles was accomplished not only because the original disciples and Paul were sent to the

Gentiles, but above all because Jesus himself, in the context of his trial, was formally "delivered over" to the Gentiles as represented by Pilate and the soldiers.

But would he whom his own people regarded as a blasphemer against God be welcome among the nations?

4. Since the days of Abraham, Jewish existence means to be a foreigner among the nations (Gen. 23:4). In the books of Exodus and Esther there are statements which remind one of recent Western "anti-Semitism"; corresponding extermination plans and pogroms were not lacking even in biblical times. Israel is unlike other nations—and is pledged not to live like them—because its Lord is unlike other Gods. When early in its history Israel yet wanted to live "like all the other nations," this desire meant the rejection of God himself (1 Sam. 8:5–8, 19–20).

Even in its distinction from other nations Israel can fulfill a beneficial function among them, as prophetic utterances from the time of the monarchy show. Seized and kicked by the two major powers of that day, i.e., Egypt and Assyria (once the symbols of "West" and "East"), this people is called not to enter political alliances with them but to become the meeting place between East and West (Isa. 7—9; 19:22–25). This way the ancient promise will be fulfilled: with the blessing given to Abraham all generations and nations will be blessed (Gen. 12:1–3; 18:18; 22:18).

According to the New Testament, Jesus dies as "the King of the Jews" and carries out a rule which "is not of this world" but is radically different from all earthly systems of government (John 18:36; Mark 10:42–45). Jesus, too, is a stranger among the great and powerful of this world. He wants only to serve (Mark 10:35–45). The love and wisdom which were revealed in his cross are, according to the standards of worldly wisdom, a scandal and a folly (1 Cor. 1:18—2:5). Pontius Pilate is amazed that the Jews themselves should hand Jesus over to his jurisdiction. He does not, however, take the strange Jew under his protection, but shrugs his shoulders, washes his hands, and lets him die—why should it bother him as long as

it is "only a Jew"? It is precisely in the illegal execution of Jesus
—which the Gospels underscore and which is not fully explained by the modern conjecture that Jesus was executed as
a kind of zealot—that Jesus was made to endure a typically
Jewish fate. No wonder that the New Testament does not promise positions of honor before princes and persons of high rank
to those who believe in Jesus, but instead, portrays the community, too, as a small band of poor people in dispersion (1 Cor.
1:26–29; Phil. 2:15; Luke 12:32; James 1:1; 1 Pet. 1:1) who must
give their testimony, if necessary, as martyrs (especially according to the Revelation of John). It is correspondingly senseless today to confront the dominance of a supposedly "white
Messiah" with the proclamation of a "black Messiah" ("Jesus
is black, baby!"). Jesus is neither an Easterner nor a Westerner
but really a Jew who is an alien in this world and yet who is
urgently needed because he is, in his weakness, the mediator
of peace.

5. Among Jesus' many characteristics and ways of behavior, which can be regarded as specifically Jewish and which are
especially extolled in the Gospels, three should be mentioned
in particular.

(a) Despite all criticism directed against Israel's self-
consciousness and the forms in which it expressed itself, Jesus
did not let himself be dissuaded from respecting the Jews as the
chosen people. He held on to "his God," even in the hour of his
death, and to the Law when he proclaimed its fulfillment by
himself and by love. Even though he had to protest against the
perversion of obedience to the Law into legalism and hypocrisy,
and himself fell victim to Sadducean jurisdiction and Pharisaic
criticism, he not only quoted up to the last minute of his life
from the Law, the Prophets, and the Psalms but he also showed
himself ready to fulfill everything. It was for him, as it is for
every Jew, self-evident that a human being is not a tragic
composite of body and soul and that he must also not consider
himself as an individual first of all, taking himself seriously
and coming to terms in whatever way with his surroundings,
but that he is body and soul a member of a community and

entrusted with responsibility for others. He also, however, did not merely live in a fundamental I-thou or dialogue relationship with his fellow human beings but, instead, in holding on to election and law, pointed to the great I, God, from whom all life derives and through whom it receives direction and destiny. He was a free human being because he knew himself to be bound only by God, because he could pray, and because he was heard. He demonstrated his freedom by showing himself to be free to serve others. He, therefore, understood election not to be a privilege and reason for pride nor the law as bondage and condemnation, but understood both as a gift and instruction for service and devotion. He thereby accomplished what every believing Jew sees as his vocation.

(b) It is characteristic of Jesus that, in his own way, he said a full yes to creation—not just to the so-called spiritual values (like those which, among his contemporaries, were given prominence by the Stoics especially) but also to the material world. We recall the birds, plants, farmers, laborers, stewards, kings that are mentioned in his parables, including their laboring and cheating, eating and drinking, producing and celebrating. Being convinced that God had made and still maintains not only the heavens and the invisible but also the earth and the tangible, he knew that everything that God had made was very good. For this reason he did not denounce the earth as a vale of tears and abandon it to its downfall. Nor did he acquiesce in the presence of sickness, demon possession or the power of death, lying, and hypocrisy. Through his deeds he "delivered" people from sickness and in his words he made clear that there are events in the world of nature and features of the common life of human beings which can serve as transparent symbols of God's promise. Like every real Jew he was convinced that God's election (the so-called "predestination") is not a soft pillow or an invitation to escape from responsible action, but calls a person to decisions and deeds—to the dutifulness of a child that is willing and ready to show its love to father, brothers, and sisters.

(c) Finally, it is typically Jewish in Jesus that his unshakable yes to his people and to human life with its hardships and joys is not sustained by a cheap optimism. He knows, rather, that the world is still unredeemed. He exposes himself to the sick, the possessed, the stupidity of his disciples, to legally sanctioned injustice, and the scorn of his despisers. He knows that we are still pilgrims in a foreign land because the history of God, of human beings, and of the world is still awaiting its fulfillment. Contrary to a widespread misunderstanding to which many theologians since Augustine have subjected the apostle Paul, Jesus did not disseminate a doctrine of original sin. An American rabbi once said to me, "In distinction to you Christians we Jews cannot take sin so seriously." Jesus showed himself to be a true Jew by proclaiming forgiveness, healing, and revival in spite of and instead of a final doom of the world. In the Revelation of John this is underscored inasmuch as one of the visions graphically describes nothing less than a new heaven *and* a new earth.

These Jewish elements in the portrait, history, and character of Jesus could be supplemented with others. However, we interrupt our enumeration in order to make room for a further elaboration of a number of those traits by which Jesus, without damage to his Jewishness, stands out as a unique figure particularly among the Jews.

IV. The Uniqueness of Jesus

Pilate called Jesus the "King of the Jews." (John 18:33, 39; 19:19, etc.) As though this were not enough, he also called the same Jesus "the man." (John 19:5) In using the words, *"Ecce homo,"* the Roman governor perhaps wanted originally to say no more than, "There, you Jews can have your fellow!" For the evangelist, however, these words meant more: Jesus is not only the king of the *Jews* whom God had promised and given, he is also *man* in the absolute sense—exactly what a human being looks like before God and is revealed by God to be. Here that which is specifically Jewish is identified with unprecedented boldness with what is universally human—perhaps also with what is all-too-human. That this one Jew, Jesus, is "human" in this absolute sense is claimed in the New Testament explicitly only in Luke 3, Romans 5, and 1 Corinthians 15, that is, in those passages in which either Jesus' descent is carried all the way back to Adam or Jesus' key position is contrasted with Adam's. But it may also be included in all texts that speak of "the Son of Man."

What is a human being? To this question, the accused, beaten Jesus who carries a crown of thorns, gives a clear answer.

1. He is a figure that does not appeal to us. He has not been chosen to be the representative either of the Jews or of "all people that on earth do dwell" through a democratic process; nor has he been chosen on the basis of the results of some Institute for Opinion Research. It was not a vote count, nor a consensus of particularly great or famous persons, nor an investigation into a collective, unconscious longing, described only in symbols, nor genuine human nature which made him what he is according to the witness of the New Testament. Rather, God has sent him (Rom. 8:3; Gal. 4:4; John 3:17, etc.), God has declared him to be his "beloved son," (Matt. 3:17; 17:5; 2 Pet. 1:17) and God has made him "Lord and Christ." (Acts 2:36; cf. Rom. 1:4) It is surprising and irritating for all people that it is precisely a Jew who is to represent the whole of humanity. He pleased the taste of no one, for he was betrayed by a Christian, Judas, then he was handed over to the Gentiles by the Jews themselves, and finally Gentiles mocked and slew him. Thus, according to the Gospel accounts all groups of humankind have looked and gone past him who was singled out by God as the truly human being. Jesus' person means for all men and women a confrontation with God's revelation: here it becomes manifest that human nature is unknown to ourselves, unless God makes it known. Already in Psalm 8:5ff. the question, "What is man?" is answered by pointing to God. Only when one speaks of God's election, care, and guidance, does light shine upon the secret of human nature and does one have cause not to despair about the riddles of suffering.

2. The man Jesus is the true human being because he

submits to the will of God in free decision. The pitiable picture which he presents to Jews and Gentiles is to be traced back to his fulfillment of the Law. Obedient men of God: prophets, kings, priests, and wise men had already existed before Jesus; even of Gentiles like Melchizedek, Cyrus, and Job it is said that they did God's will. But the fulfillment of God's instruction by Jesus is different from all anticipations. "Here is more than Solomon" (Luke 11:31)—for the following reasons:

(a) Jesus never understood either written or orally transmitted laws as a summons to casuistry, ceremonialism, or to selective or partial obedience which might be called *pars pro toto*. He knew that God—as Paul would say—cannot be put off with "works of the law" and that no person can become justified before God by his own accomplishments. He did, however, in the midst and for the benefit of an unbelieving, rebellious, and hate-filled generation, hold onto the institution and the core of the Law. He "came to fulfill it," "to fulfill it in us," and to be its "fulfillment" (not to be its termination, Matthew 5:17; Rom. 8:4; 10:4) by believing in God and by loving his neighbor (also his enemies!). Just as an Old Testament king or other servant of God could "by his righteousness obtain righteousness for many" by interceding for them (Isa. 53:11–12), so Jesus Christ's faith and love are an act of intercession before God, as a representative event by which "many" are made just before God. "Man," who since Adam has fallen under the power of sin and of death, has been moved into a new light and a new status since the coming of Jesus Christ. Now he may know and hope that he will not have to stand before God only as a damned sinner but may stand there also as just ("justified").

(b) The price which Jesus paid for his obedience, his faith, and his love consists in his death. "Obedient unto death," love unto "death for the friends" (Phil. 2:8; John 15:13; Gal. 1:4, 2:20; Eph. 5:2, 25)—this is the criterion to which he submits. Jesus fulfilled the Law not only actively but also passively in that he allowed to happen to him what was threatened to all transgressors of God's will. He took upon himself the death of one who had been cursed and abandoned by God. The Letter to the

Galatians (3:13) actually speaks of the "curse" of God, i.e. of an eternal rejection, which is different from the wrath of God because that flames up only for a short time. It is true that rebels and breakers of the covenant were threatened with this curse in the Old Testament (especially in Deuteronomy), but one cannot say, even in the face of the most severe blows which both individuals in Israel and the entire chosen people suffered, that the curse was ever carried out. However, Jesus with the crown of thorns, Jesus on the cross, shows the true human condition before God. Here is the "accursed Jew" who himself bears what all human beings should have deserved.

(c) The purpose of the giving of the Law was to place the people of Israel under a discipline which would qualify this people to be the bearer of the blessing, that is, to be a priest and a light among the nations of the Gentiles (Gen. 12:1–3; Exod. 19:5–6; Isa. 42:6). Election, Law, and obedience were never an end in themselves—as though, for example, the Jews ought to be or could be better people than other human beings. Jesus fulfilled Israel's purpose by not only showing a concern in individual instances for Gentile people but by conducting himself in such a way that he was "handed over" to the Gentiles. The result of *his* extradition was the spreading of the blessing, of the knowledge of God, of faith, of love among the Gentiles, the "gospel" which, as the mission was carried out, brought about the establishment of "congregations of God" throughout the world. The Jew Jesus became the "savior" and "light of the world." Thus salvation did indeed come "from the Jews." (John 4:22, 42; 8:12)

This breakthrough to the Gentiles, however, did not happen without the resurrection, about which we now need to speak explicitly.

3. Only Jesus among all Jews has been raised to new and eternal life almost immediately after his death. It is crucial to note that none other than the crucified was resurrected: he who was and still is disparaged by the majority of humankind, and who was rejected for three days by God. This was an earth-shaking event which proved Jesus to be the one person on earth

with whom God was well pleased and to whom full power over all people and all created things is given (Matt. 28:18-20; Phil. 2:9-11). This resurrection and enthronement are unique; they must not be reduced to the level of mere symbols that are applicable to every private or national aspiration. (There are, for instance, individual Jewish voices today saying that after the horrors of Auschwitz the foundation of the State of Israel is a kind of resurrection. Arabic, even Moslem, poets do not want to lag behind when they sing about the pains and hopes of the Palestinian people and describe the rise of the Palestinian self-awareness, now awakening after centuries of oppression, as a resurrection from the cross.) What is the historical, literal, and spiritual sense which the words "cross" and "resurrection" have when they are concatenated as closely as is the case in the New Testament descriptions and confessions of Jesus Christ? Whereas a human being in the Old Testament (like Saul or David) is either chosen or rejected, the New Testament shows that the rejected Jesus is also God's chosen one. There is here no longer a "double predestination" in the sense that one is either "not loved" or "loved." Rather, from Easter there shines a radiant light not only over the cross of Jesus but on the suffering of every human being, whether Jew or Gentile. It is now over with the pride of the *in-group* which despises the people in the *out-group*. It is also over with the narcissistic self-pity of chosen persons who imagine that they are treated unjustly by God and humankind or of *outsiders* who imagine that they are robbed of all chances and see themselves condemned to existence in a dark corner. It was precisely the beloved who accepted God's chastisement. Both God's suffering on account of rebellious humanity and our own well-deserved suffering he took upon himself and endured. By the resurrection God reveals his grace over all humankind, even the seemingly godforsaken people. He vindicates them and gives meaning to their lives. The justification and glorification of the life "for others," of service to the suffering human being, occurred signally in the resurrection of the Jew Jesus.

It is true that a justification and glorification of human

existence is also proclaimed or sought after on a humanistic or
Marxist basis. Still, humanistic arguments cannot get by without strict moral, e.g., Stoic conditions and demands. Also "the
new man" whom Marxist ideology and praxis claim to create
and shape has as yet not been demonstrated to be different
from a utopia. The New Testament, however, announces a fact
and a gift: in the midst of the old and torn humanity, suffering
from distress, the new human being has become historical reality. While many may still deny that the crucified and resurrected Jesus is this "new man," we have reason to trust the
explicit biblical promise that his unique position as guarantor
of the justification of "human beings" will yet be acknowledged
worldwide. The same Jesus Christ will appear in glory at his
return.

Humanity's future, and thereby also its present, is determined by the coming of God in the figure of the exalted Son of
Man, who is the Son of God and the son of the Jewess Mary at
the same time.

V. Conclusion

The Jews are right in not wanting us to form arbitrary
opinions of them in order then to show them appropriate hon-
ors or to impose burdens upon them. We should ask about their
self-understanding which is often different from our understanding of them. I am aware that in the preceding discussion
I have brought together from the Bible and other books, also
from conversations and experiences, certain things which to
Jewish ears sound more *or less* correct and important. The
many sages among the Jews know that they, too, are not
finished with the study and understanding of Jesus.

I would like to state under three aspects the kinds of decisions Christians are called to make today.

(1) We cannot believe in Jesus without rendering love and
loyalty to the people out of which he comes, which he represents, and whose mission among the other peoples he confirmed
for all time. If God had become untrue to his chosen people by
sending and resurrecting Jesus Christ, then he might also

someday become untrue to us Gentiles. The father of the two lost sons (Luke 15:11 ff.) shows himself to be a faithful and dependable father by turning to the older one just as totally and graciously as to the younger. Because God himself, by old and new prophets, is still upholding the mission of and to the Jews, we Gentile Christians are relieved of the illusion that the Jews are now the abandoned and lost ones and that it is up to us to convert them. After Auschwitz and the earlier church-supported pogroms our only task is to be penitent and let ourselves be converted.

(2) We see all Jews, whether they be orthodox, zealots, or atheists, militant Zionists or philanthropic benefactors in the dispersion, in indissoluble unity with Jesus Christ. Auschwitz meant that we contributed to the crucifixion of Christ. The intervention by Jews on behalf of social justice, their generosity, their joy in work, their orientation toward a new heaven and a new earth, and their steadfastness in suffering shame us. Often they carry out what was entrusted to the church. Their survival and their security, whether in the State of Israel or in the dispersion, is essential for the continuing existence and faith of the church if the church is not to become a pagan cultic and social institution but rather is to represent together with the Jews the one people of God on earth.

(3) Church and everyday worship can only exist in secret solidarity with the worship in synagogues and Jewish homes. Baptism became the sign of entrance into the church because originally it was a sign of penitence within Israel. The communion meal is the fulfillment of the Passover Meal. Every time that Jews are penitent on the Day of Atonement we too are called on to be penitent. When, during the Passover Meal, they wait for the one who is to come, we wait with them. Even though in the First Letter to the Thessalonians, under the impact of the harsh persecution of the community by Jewish authorities, Paul speaks harsh words against the Jews, and although in the Letters to the Romans and Galatians he deals with the temporary breaking away and casting out of the Jews (1 Thess. 2:14–16; Rom. 11:17–21; Gal. 4:30), we Gentiles know

that we belong to the one people of God only because we are naturalized citizens in Israel (Eph. 2:13–19) and because we wait with the Jews for the *one* shepherd of *one* flock. It is not possible to serve God in the name of Jesus Christ and to separate oneself from the Jews.

This means that just as Jesus in the time of the New Testament signified a crisis and a call to salvation and life for Judaism, so today the Jew Jesus is the criterion, the judgment, but also God's call to salvation for the predominantly Gentile-Christian church, its theology, and its course of conduct.

ISRAEL
AND
THE PALESTINIANS

ISRAEL AND
THE PALESTINIANS

Introduction

The topic "Israel and the Palestinians" is a controversial one. Anyone dealing with it must be aware that one can make enemies of anybody who is concerned with religion and politics in the Near East: Jews living within or without the State of Israel, Arabs and Palestinians, Christians and non-Christians in or outside the Near East. Everything that I would like to present for reflection and discussion about the troubles and temptations of the State of Israel and of the Palestinians is intended as an address to friends of Israel such as those coming together in Christian-Jewish study groups. It is also an appeal to Jews both in and outside of the land of Israel who do not belong to such study groups and consider these "inter-faith conversations" as ill-advised and even meaningless today.

During recent years, both when I have become acquainted with and when I have been invited to address Arabs (both Christian and non-Christian), Palestinians, and leftist groups that are hostile to Israel, I have presented a message that differs from the perspective which I suggest now. On those occasions I was reviled as a hard-boiled Zionist who, together with Western ecclesiastical circles, misuses the Bible in order to provide the existence and policies of Israel with an undeserved halo.

I cannot, however, serve the friends of the State of Israel if I only try to gloss over serious problems or shower them with extravagant praise. Rather, I need to deal clearly with those problems and tasks which present themselves to Israel and the church, but especially to a Christian-Jewish study group. It is all too cheap to find fault with those who are absent at the moment and to expect only of them a reversal of direction and a new orientation. What needs to occupy our attention is *our* guilt, not theirs. For this reason I expect understanding and patience—even if one should get the impression in what follows that the boat is occasionally leaning to one side.

The sources from which I have derived my information and evaluation of the situation are of varied kinds. In America I carried on for fifteen years an intensive and friendly exchange of views with scholarly as well as with popular rabbis, with synagogue and temple congregations, with Jewish and Jewish-Christian agencies. In Switzerland I am trying to do no differently. Twice I have been to Israel and once to Beirut. Not only were doors opened wide by Jewish, Arab, and Palestinian dignitaries, but I also attempted to listen to the voice of the famous, at times legendary, "man of the street." At the same time, I was aware of the chance character of all information available to a visitor. I cannot remember the number of conferences and consultations attended. Still, personal encounters and experiences would be too narrow and fortuitous for serious evaluation. The study of written materials is the second leg on which I stand—all the way from statistical data (which are grossly contradictory depending on their origin) to books, journalistic productions, printed or duplicated essays, consultation or travel reports, demagogic speeches, and written detailed statements from parties immediately involved in the conflict. I have to admit a gap in the acquaintance with materials stemming from Egypt, Jordan, and Syria. The reading especially of propaganda literature, which often includes books that are clothed in scientific or belletristic garments, is no pleasure. But it supplements the impression of boiling emotion and passion with which even educated persons on both sides defend their information and conclusions. Taking the transrational actions and reactions seriously is part of understanding the existing tensions—and part also of an effort to contribute to an easing of tension which might someday lead to peace.

The easiest way to organize what is now going to be discussed is to distinguish simply between *facts* about which the Israeli and Palestinian sides are agreed, the *image* (i.e., the self-understanding) of each partner in the conflict, and the *enemy-image* that each holds about the other or that is attributed to him by others. All three of these categories must obviously be held in mind each step of the way. Whenever I have to use controversial formulations, I intend to name the source from which they are derived.

There are, however, two things which make it impossible to use the three categories just mentioned as a clear-cut principle of organization. (a) Even the existing image and enemy-image are a part of the facts; utopias as well as errors and lies possess a relative degree of reality. Facts and images, therefore, cannot always be sharply separated from each other. (b) It can hardly be expected that either an Israeli Jew or a Palestinian can do anything other than regard his or her self-image and enemy-image as "true" and those of the opponent as "false." A third person may be able in individual cases to prefer this or that "view" of things or to declare solidarity with one of the two sides. I myself cannot in any case proceed on the assumption that one side is *always* right and the other is *always* wrong. God alone is and remains judge.

There is one additional preliminary consideration which needs to be taken up although it cannot be expressed all in one breath. It has to do with limiting the topic. Would it not be most useful for future peace in the Near East—as a rabbi and a pastor from Bern have actually proposed—if, instead of the emotion-laden problem of "Israel and the Palestinians," only the relationship between "Israel and Its Arab Fellow-Citizens" were to be dealt with? This proposal arose out of the conviction that the "Arabs" who had been naturalized citizens of Israel since 1948 constituted a model for a future peaceful relationship between the groups which today are still enemies. Indeed, an "Arab" group does exist inside the State of Israel; it is a vital part of the state. But is its factual inclusion also a solution of the problem posed by its distinct character?

Several comments are necessary in order to show how difficult it is to answer this question. The concept "Israel" has several meanings not only today but also in the Bible.

(a) It can designate God's chosen people (Abraham, Isaac, and Jacob as representatives of the nation which was constituted under Moses, Joshua, the Judges, and the early Kings) as against the people who once have been rejected (Ishmael and his descendants). For Jews and Christians only Israel, therefore, means the same as "chosen people." The Moslems, however, consider themselves to be descendants of Ishmael. They retain greatest respect for their ancestor Ibrahim (Abraham) and his undefiled monotheistic faith. All biblical patriarchs are held in high esteem; this is evident by their mention in the Koran and the veneration of their tombs in the Mosque at Hebron. Even Moses and the Prophets (and Jesus) count as precursors of Mohammed. But since the disappointment which Mohammed suffered in Medina after 622 A.D. when the local Jews did not recognize him as the Last Prophet, only the Moslems are considered as God's true people, while Jews and Christians are at best tolerated as not yet enlightened persons. Some (late?) passages in the Koran contain hints that Ishmael rather than Isaac was to be sacrificed by Abraham on Mount Moriah, while only one text speaks of the blessing given to the Eastern and Western (=Palestinian) parts of the earth which are given to the weakened children of Israel. At any rate, the election is no longer considered a privilege of "Israel." All who insist upon the continued unique role of Israel are suspect of denying the Arabs, if not all Moslems, the right to exist. They are considered unfit to contribute to a reconciliation between Jews and Arabs.

(b) An anticipation of a very different conflict is equally present in the Bible. "Israel" is not only a name for the entire people but also for the Northern Kingdom, which came into being after Solomon's death, in contrast to the Judaean Southern Kingdom. A tension within the chosen people, comparable to the words of the apostle Paul, "Not all who are descended from Israel belong to Israel," (Rom. 9:6) thus is indicated. In contrast to Judah, Israel appears to be rejected. The prophets of the exile, however, declare just as emphatically as Paul does later on that the internal tension will not last *eternally* because

someday one flock under one shepherd will be raised up, gath-
ered, and redeemed (Ezek. 34 and 37; Rom. 11:25–32; cf. John
10:16).

This *biblical* diversity, dialectics, and dynamics of the concept "Israel" are being increased today and have been made
particularly complex by various *political* meanings of the same
word. The Jewish state which was founded on May 14, 1948
chose for itself the name "Israel." The territory provided for
this state by the United Nations in New York during November 1947 was more limited than the actual borders which were
won in battle by the new state in the War of 1948. The greater
portion of the Arab citizens of Israel came into Israel neither
through the decision of the United Nations nor through self-
determination. In any case, Israel calls itself today a "Jewish
state" even though among its three million citizens there are
450,000 "Arab," 40,000 Drusian, and 2,000 Czerkessian inhabitants. The birth rate among the Arab "fellow-citizens" is much
higher than that of the Jews. Despite a frightening number of
Jewish emigrants from Israel, the ongoing large immigration
of Jews from all over the world into Israel—particularly from
Russia—has so far helped to maintain the Jewish majority's
solid proportion of six to one.

In the Six-Day War of June 1967 Israel succeeded in con-
quering territories from the Suez Canal to the Golan Heights.
Despite repeated protests of the United Nations (especially in
the Resolutions 242 and 338), certain areas in and around
Jerusalem were submitted in every regard to Israel's civic administration; in other words, they were annexed. The largest
portion, however, is even today, according to official language,
"held" or "occupied"; in the language of Israel's rightist parties
it is "liberated." Israel bears now the poor esteem, even the
hatred, which any occupying power has to bear because of both,
the feelings of the controlled, expelled, and fugitive population,
and the reaction of world opinion. Among the Arabs there is
the apprehension not only of a solidification of Israel's hold on
the controlled areas but even of farther expansion. Grandiose
statements and threats which are made in the Knesset and

other gatherings, in newspapers and in the streets, by highly
vocal representatives of a "greater" or even of "Great Israel"
show that this fear is not ungrounded. Accordingly from 1967
on for Jewish Israelis the word "Israel" means a state which is
struggling with all its strength for peace and secure borders.
For most Arabs and for Palestinians the same term denotes a
power structure which is robustly vigorous, dynamic, and ex-
plosive, hardly capable of keeping imperialist tendencies con-
cealed in its own ranks.

We shall employ the term "Israel" from this point on in its
present-day political sense, but not in its biblical meaning of
the chosen People of God. That is, we are talking about the
State of Israel. At the same time, we cannot forget under any
circumstances that his state is made up of a majority consisting
of Jews—in other words, of people who according to the Bible
and our faith are placed in a special way under the protection
and judgment of God. They are and remain called of God to be
the first-born and prototype among all nations. "Has God rejected his people? Far from it!" (Rom. 11:1ff.)

What are we, however, to think of the expression, "Israel's
Arab fellow-citizens"? This term may sound good, but it contains and covers up problems that are not a matter of numbers.
The term "fellow-citizen" may, indeed, enable some well-
known spokesmen for the Palestinians (among them the former Greek-Catholic Archbishop Raya of Galilee) to designate
Israel as "our state" and to acknowledge, particularly in times
of war, their full solidarity with this state. The equality of
rights for all citizens regardless of religion, race, or origin,
including freedom in matters of faith, conscience, education,
language, and culture was solemnly proclaimed by David Ben
Gurion on the day of the founding of the state. The Palestinians
living in Israel have participated in the development of this
state, especially as indispensible co-workers in the progress
made in Israel's agriculture and industry as well as in its edu-
cational and health systems. Their voice can be heard in the
Knesset. They work hard and they profit when the output in-
creases and wages are improved. With the Jews they groan

under the burden of taxes. The large majority of them hate war
and acts of terrorism; they want nothing more than peace. As
long as one looks only at the amount of money which goes
through their hands or at the development of productivity,
homes, and health care, the Israeli view is defensible: the Palestinian Arabs have never had it so good as now in and under the
Jewish state.

Still, not all Arab citizens of Israel share the views of the
Archbishop referred to earlier who, at the instigation of his
church, was forced to relinquish his position in the fall of 1974.
There are two decisive reasons for this:

1. The concept of "fellow-citizen" has a reverse side. What
would an Appalachian hillbilly think of the topic "The U.S.A.
and Fellow-Citizens from the Appalachian Mountains," or
what would a handicapped person think of the title, "Healthy
People and Their Handicapped Fellow Human Beings"? Such
formulations reveal a prejudice on the part of the majority
towards a less privileged minority. An undertone of condescen-
sion is clearly audible—at least for the less fortunate or weaker
part of the society. Sensitive Israeli citizens are aware that
even the Western Jews' references to their "oriental brothers
of Eastern (Ashkenazi) origin" have a mean character.

Although many Palestinians are actually "fellow-citizens"
in Israel, only Jews are really to be regarded as full "citizens."
De jure or *de facto,* access to the army, to university studies,
and to the higher administrative offices is not open to an Arab-
Palestinian "fellow-citizen" in the same way as it is to a Jewish
"citizen." Perhaps the exclusion from the army is meant to
include a humanitarian element: Israel will not force Arabs to
shoot at brothers. But since the politically less suspect Druses
are welcome in the Israeli armed forces, an intended discrimi-
nation against the Arabs cannot be excluded. The latter is
obvious in other fields: there exists an Israeli "Law of Return"
granting the right of immigration and naturalization to every
Jew in the whole world. But this Law does not speak of the
Palestinian fellow-citizen's son, brother, or father who before
or after 1948 fled or was expelled to Jordan, Lebanon, Egypt,

Iraq, etc. In the almost thirty years of Israeli statehood, no more than about 40,000 persons who had left their homeland of their own will or under pressure, have been repatriated under a program of family-reunion. At all levels of higher education the culture gap between Western Jews and Palestinian manual workers explains only partly the low percentage of Palestinian students at, e.g., the Hebrew University in Jerusalem. But it is to be acknowledged that on the national level the number of Palestinian students tripled between 1968 and 1973. Though some small and large Palestinian business enterprises have profited from the Jewish political presence, there are others which have succumbed to Israeli competition not because of the lacking capacities of their owners but by lack of protection from arbitrary restrictions and harassments.

Since the State of Israel is itself "Jewish"—not as a political entity tied to a specific religion but as a state governed primarily by Jews and intended for Jews—one may ask whether the "Arab fellow-citizens" really are more than permanent foreign workers or tolerated settlers. Equality before the law on paper does not always correspond to equality of civil rights. The good will shown by Teddy Kollek, the mayor of Jerusalem, to the Arab population and some statutes issued to protect the rights of the latter are sometimes frustrated and contradicted by measures taken by the national government. In present-day Israel, the majority of citizens rejoice over every Arab fellow-citizen who emigrates, but are sorry to see certain Israelis leave the land. Despite great difficulties, a Jew from Russia may find it easier to migrate to Israel than a Palestinian from Israel to be admitted to the U.S.A. or to Iraq. So much about the actual *in*equality of the Arab fellow-citizens.

2. Though tolerant and open-minded Jews who oppose the language chosen in the Israeli right wing quarters, use the expressions "Arab" or "Arabic," this nomenclature is misleading. "If a war breaks out again," I was assured in 1972 by a Palestinian on a street in Jerusalem's Old City, "we shall fight first of all against the Arabs, only then against the Israelis." This attitude is hardly general and will certainly change as

soon as new political stances are chosen by Arab states. Still, a certain resentment among Palestinians against their classification as Arabs deserves to be respected.

When, of course, voices from Beirut, Damascus, Cairo, etc. tell the Palestinians that their salvation comes from *arabité* they cannot refuse the solidarity and help offered. The common Arabic language indicates a cultural coherence, and this cohesion is buttressed by religion and poetry. Islam has always claimed to be the bond unifying all Arabs; the Arabs, in turn, have been called "the raw material of Islam." Even today, religion, culture, social life, and politics form an inseparable whole among them. Therefore the struggle against the yoke of colonial powers and for political freedom and unity expresses concerns that are as much Arabic as Moslemic. However, unlike his predecessor Nasser who had made strong appeals for the unification of all Arabs, President Sadat, in fall 1977, started his daring peace initiative by denying the Arab character of the Egyptians. While more Arab states move to making Islam their state religion, Sadat has so far attempted to cut back the influence of Moslem chauvinists. Thus he has alienated almost all Arab powers from himself—while he still supports Palestinian hopes for an independent state of their own.

The political and social programs of the PLO and other refugee organizations put freedom and independence rather than *arabité* and/or Islam in the foreground. When Israeli speeches and decrees speak of an "Arab" potion of the Israeli population they express a political judgment but do not solve the problem. The large majority of non-Jews who have migrated into Palestine from Arab territories ever since the twenties have as little contact with their countries of origin as the blacks in America have with Africa.

In any case, actions and inactions, trouble and promise of the Palestinians cannot simply be identified with the success or failure of the Arab nations. We venture the statement: the wars which thus far have been waged between Israel and its Arab neighbors were not (with the exception of the invasions into Lebanese territory) wars against or for the Palestinians.

The Arab states fought for their own interests, not for the Palestinians. Israel fought for its survival in the sea of Arab nations, not against the Palestinians as such—but, in 1978, Israel did fight against the PLO Palestinians. The Palestinians stand humanly, legally, morally, and politically alone—completely alone between the Israeli hammer and the Arab anvil. These reasons should suffice to explain why the topic, "Israel and Its Arab Fellow-Citizens" contains so many biased prejudgments that it really appears to be useful only for Israeli governmental authorities and their propaganda.

We shall first describe Israel, then the Palestinians. Finally we shall raise the question whether the revelation of the God of Abraham, the Father of our Lord Jesus Christ, provides us with a definite position and function in the present conflict.

I. Israel

The State of Israel was born in 1948 in an emergency and has always existed ever since in a state of emergency. It was intended as a fulfillment of the over 2500 years-old longing of many Jews for a return to their land, as an alternative to the assimilation of Jews into the nations among whom they lived in dispersion, as a secure home for those who like Colonel Dreyfus had come to discover their foreignness in an allegedly enlightened and tolerant Western society. Finally, and above all, this state was supposed to offer lasting security to all those who had survived the deathcamps of Auschwitz and Maidenek and hoped to find protection from further pogroms. If it were not for the longing of many Jews to be able finally to exist in freedom as Jews, and if for all Jews it were not a question of life or death, namely, of survival in a demonstrably Jews-hating and Jews-murdering world, there would be no State of Israel today.

The State of Israel has, however, brought no one the security which had been hoped for. Neither the Palestinians nor the neighboring Arab countries were prepared to pay the price for the appalling attitude of the churches and nations of Europe. Thus every one of the four wars since 1948, but also every terrorist act before or after the founding of the state, has made it clear to the Jews who have returned home that even in the land of their fathers they are still unsafe aliens, i.e., still in exile (galut). A single war lost, a single demonstration of real weakness could mean for Israel that, with the extinction of the State of Israel, the Jewish population would be exposed to a massacre as, indeed, has several times been announced by radical voices. However, it seems that the Arab neighbors of Israel can easily survive incompetent governments and lost battles.

It has been of limited use to Israel that, owing to its exceptionally well-armed, well-trained, and brave military forces, it has won wars. Even if it had been as victorious in October 1973 as it had been in 1948, 1956, and 1967, the external as well as internal threats to its security would only have grown. The Arab nations would have prepared for the next round but Israel in the meantime would have had to administer even more occupied territories and to keep under control or to expel even more Palestinians. It would thereby have found itself between Scylla and Charybdis. (a) If, following suggestions made in the Knesset before the Six-Day War, it would expand its boundaries to the precincts of Cairo and Damascus, it would eventually have to grant some sort of citizenship to more and more non-Jewish people and thus reduce the proportion of the Jewish majority, which at any rate is menaced by the population increase of the "Arabs." In the foreseeable future Jews would be a minority in Great-Israel. (b) If Israel chose to treat the population of the occupied areas as disenfranchised subjects, permanent suspects of irredentist feelings and movements, or a mere reservoir of laborers (in other words, as a Bantu state), it could in the long run not claim to be a modern democratic state; it would have become a companion of South Africa, Rhodesia, and those younger African states in which the government seems to serve primarily the rule of one tribe over the others.

Up to this time the several governments and the changing majorities in the Knesset of Israel have neither sought nor seized an opportunity to demonstrate how a peaceful co-existence of the Jews with the Palestinians would work. Is this a tragic necessity caused by the as yet existing state of war with its neighbors? Is it an oversight or shortcoming in the setting of priorities which in the light of achievements in other fields ought not be dragged into the foreground? Or is it Israel's share in that nationalistic plague to which in one form or another all nations succumb? Certainly, only persons and states who pretend to have clean hands in the treatment of minorities might be willing to speak of plain guilt and to throw the first stones.

However, there are many indications that Israel has missed many opportunities since 1948, especially in Galilee, to show by positive example, how it understands the equality of its Palestinian citizens before the law. It was a world-famous American rabbi who first drew my attention to the fact that former and present plans and steps in favor of a "Judaization of Galilee" discourage even those among the Palestinians who are willing fully to recognize the Jewish state and to cooperate with it. In 1976, Israel Koenig, District Commissioner of Galilee in the service of the Interior Ministry, produced a secret policy paper "blunt and laden with anti-Arab racism" which "stunned many of Israel's Jews—and outraged all of its Arabs." (*Newsweek International*, Sept. 27, 1976, p. 18) Reduction of employment facilities and of children's subsidies for large families, also encouragement of pressures on "Arab" businesses and of the emigration of Palestinians were among the measures proposed. Though this drastic proposal was not accepted by the government but declared a most unfortunate private opinion, Koenig was permitted to retain his position. The enormous increase of the Jewish population in Galilee since 1948, (from about 10 to over 50%), the successive disappearance of the Palestinian pockets; and the lack of anything approximating cultural or socio-political autonomy reveal what is going on. In vain were the Palestinian protests made on the "Day of the Earth." And yet there are Israeli and Jewish voices which assert that "Israel does not need to reprove itself for nor be ashamed of anything that concerns its behavior towards the Palestinians." They also describe the policies of the occupation forces in West Jordan as the "most humane of all time." The opinions about themselves held by those who happen to be the stronger are always favorable—but seldom if ever are they decisive for those who are the weaker of two groups.

The unsolved Palestinian problem and the peril which arises from the external threat to Israel's existence is coupled with a state of emergency in the nation's domestic political life. Israel, of course, possesses a parliament, a government, an army, an efficient administrative system and it can point to great economic and cultural achievements. Still it does not yet have a constitution. This means, as will be shown later, that the government, the administrators, and the army can disregard any decisions of the Supreme Court. The reason for this deficiency is to be found in the inner disunity of the Jewish citizens themselves. Pious and fully secularized Jews, Sephardic and Ashkenazi Jews, Jews from Yemen and from Frankfurt, new arrivals and old settlers, militant chauvinists and pacifist sectarians, cool intellectuals and hysterical masses, white beards, military haircuts, and the long hair of young people face each other across a chasm of distrust. There are Jewish Israelis who, for religious reasons, do not consider the contemporary state to be a "Jewish" state; they feel incapable of equating the larger and smaller immigration waves from the dispersion with the promised return. Although there have always been tensions between the Jews in exile and those in the homeland, today the clash between the returnees and the residents or early settlers is even stronger. Even among the Jews it is regarded as a miracle that this state not only should have come into existence but should continue to exist.

While it is true that the much advertised "Arab unity" needs the sting of Israel's presence and the Palestinian problem in order to find a shape and to be continued, elements of truth may also be found in the accusation of Israel's enemies, saying that Israel needs the continuation of the state of war if only to prevent it from tearing itself to pieces. Still there is much more truth to Ben Gurion's word, "whoever does not believe in miracles is not a realist." The absence of a constitution, however, does mean a continuing insecurity, legally speaking, for the Palestinian fellow-citizens.

Israel's peril is not reduced by the fact that it has only one strong friend: the United States of America. Only in a few instances has the majority of Jews or of the Israelis praised the United Nations Organization as a protector of Israel—e.g., when the United Nations in November of 1947 decided on the partition of Palestine or when in the spring of 1948 it contributed to the rescue of the Jews living and fighting in Jerusalem by mediating an armistice. However, because the Security Council has since then repeatedly condemned Israeli aggression, occupation, and annexation, the Jews have felt themselves abandoned by the United Nations. For a long time they have thrown themselves into the arms of the Americans—the same United States which, before and during the Vietnam War, had shown the face of a crude imperialistic power and had called forth, by the methods it employed in its fighting, the protest of almost the whole world—but not of the government of Israel or of General Moshe Dayan who "as a journalist" visited the American army in Vietnam.

It is true that Israel's friendship with the U.S.A. provided financial, military, tactical, and political support for the young state. But an enormous price was paid for this friendship. Even in the beginning of the fifties and after the unfortunate Sinai campaign of 1956 at the latest, Russia saw its interests in the Near East threatened—with the result that it joined the Arab enemies of Israel (despite its earlier opposite attitude) or attempted to assume leadership over them. In the West not only did the New Left but also the All-Christian Peace Conference in Sagorsk (1967) declare Israel to be an exponent of capitalism and colonialism. I consider this "Marxist Analysis of History" to be one-sided, but it is also widespread in the Third World. Yehuda Magnes and Martin Buber had worked for a binational state on the territory of the former Palestine; many socialist ideals were to be realized in it. If these two great thinkers were still alive today, they would be as alarmed and distressed about the development of their nation as is true of many a sincere Jew in Israel, in America, and also in Europe.

What, however, is the situation with respect to Israel's security in view of the tendencies just mentioned? Understandably, in view of the external and internal emergencies facing the state, the idea of "national security" plays a major role in discussions at higher or lower levels. It is surprising, however, that as yet government, parliament, and people have allowed the definition and implementation of this "security" to be handled solely by generals and policemen, rather than by those responsible for foreign and domestic politics. How can anyone, in this age of parachute troops, rocket bombs, and jet airplanes still talk of "secure borders?" Is it reasonable to believe in methods for combatting terrorists and insurgents which have consistently failed since the time of the British mandate, and have proven to be ineffective in Vietnam and Mozambique?

We have already said that after Auschwitz "survival" had to become one of the most compelling motivations for all Jews. Since the Israelis were faced with the threat of consistent harassment by terrorist actions that could eventually lead to annihilation, they allowed the concept of "survival" to be transformed and eventually replaced with the term "national security." But these two words have an ominous ring, for they have been misused by aggressive major and minor powers all over the globe, and were particularly prominent in Richard Nixon's manipulation of internal politics. Even so, neither the implementation of suppressive measures in the name of "national security" by generals nor Israel's continued hold on the occupied territories has achieved the desired goal. The enormous percentage of both the gross national income and the financial contributions and loans from abroad spent on military expenditures along with the burden of the unending state of almost total mobilization on the soldiers and their relatives prevent the Israeli Jews from pursuing other peaceful ends. In fact, this preoccupation contributes to the suffering of the Palestinians.

Three examples may illustrate why in particular those "fellow-citizens" who have a great interest in a peaceful future for Israel see in the existing security measures nothing else but a curtailment or an obliteration of their rights.

1. The most blatant instance is the treatment of the two Palestinian villages Ikrit and Bir Am near the Lebanese border. Because it is little known and scarcely mentioned I would like to give a brief sketch of its history. In connection with the establishment of the State of Israel in 1948, Christian Palestinians, who before 1948 had given ample proof of their sympathy with the Jews, had to evacuate these villages for military reasons. They were promised that they would be allowed to return after the end of hostilities. When this promise was not kept, the ousted residents of the two villages sued in the law courts against the military orders. In 1952 the Supreme Court of Israel decided in their favor. The Israeli army answered the court's verdict by blowing up the vacant houses of Ikrit and Bir Am sparing only the churches and graveyards, and by forcibly preventing the return of the property owners to the ruins. In spite of vigorous protests, Golda Meir's government in 1972 defended the steps taken by the military. To this day the residents have not been permitted to return to their villages. The land belonging to the villages was added to three near-by agricultural settlements, two large kibbutzim and one moshab. Like Naboth long ago in his struggle with King Ahab for his vineyard (1 Kings 21), the majority of the previous owners refused to accept any compensation. Those among them who have not found a different kind of occupation are today "allowed" during the daytime to work as day-laborers on their former property. Measures taken in recent years to expropriate Bedouin land near Nablus and near Rafiah in the Gaza strip and to rent "for archaeological purposes" settlement space near Shilo were equally unjust. In biblical language this means that there are Palestinians who are permitted as citizens and under Israeli rule to keep body and soul together as "hewers of wood and drawers of water." Expressed in modern language this means that *de facto* those fellow-citizens who are already present or who are viewed as prospective ones by the advocates of a "Greater Israel" are really second-class citizens. No less a person than the former adviser to the prime minister for Arab

Affairs, Shmuel Toledano—who threatened to resign at several occasions and is now a member of the Knesset—has made this point explicitly. Well-known Jewish professors and writers, in and outside of Israel at protest rallies and actions, have expressed their views in opposition to the treatment of the "Two Villages"—hitherto without success. A Jewish lady from Tel Aviv who is actively engaged in the quest for healing this still bleeding wound writes, "Only a Jew in the Diaspora may understand, why those people desire to return to their 'own home.' " Still, according to Palestinian data, about 250 (a far less reliable source augmented the figure to "over 500") Palestinian villages disappeared from the earth on Israel's territory between 1948 and 1967.

2. The next example has to do with the occupation of areas outside the national borders of 1948–67. Palestinian citizens and refugees have noticed that *one* definition among others of "secure borders" means borders which make it impossible to fire on Israeli settlements within sight. For they have observed that, in every instance no later than twenty-four hours after the occupation of a part of the Golan Heights, a Jewish military settlement was established—a locality, in other words, which was inhabited by civilians also and which in turn was exposed to direct fire. I admit that I can easily understand those Palestinians who have asked themselves in wonderment how much more territory Israel still intends to conquer in order to acquire "secure borders." Is this term really anything else than a cover for expansionist plans which (on the basis of a false translation of Genesis 15:18) call for the securing of living space "from the Nile to the Euphrates" for the 14 million Jews who are still dispersed around the world? However fantastic and implausible such thinking may sound to all sensible people, the anxiety over this among Palestinians, Syrians, Iraqis, Lebanese, Jordanians, Egyptians is substantiated by the dominant influence of the super-Zionist Ariel Sharon in the Israeli government. Since the Law of Return, which has been proclaimed for the benefit of *all* Jews in the world, today is combined with the striking power of an army which is prepared for *all* security

measures, one can readily understand the mood of panic found among those who so often have been defeated, particularly, however, among the Palestinians. Even if it is exaggerated, it continues to be a reality. It is precisely the Law of Return (which a Jewish state can hardly be expected to revoke) that constitutes for the Palestinians the heart of the problem: the real threat to their life, their dignity, their property. Not until Henry Kissinger secured, under massive threats, a withdrawal of Israeli forces from the shores of the Suez Canal and from Kuneitra on the Golan Heights was there a promising beginning of Israeli moderation. It was furthermore, a good sign that, with the beginning of Yitzhak Rabin's administration, the Israeli army has several times prevented the illegal establishment of Jewish settlements on the West Bank. All the more it is regrettable that Menachem Begin's government decided in the summer of 1977 to increase the number of settlements far beyond the sixty-five to seventy (in 1976).

3. The third example does not come from occupied areas alone. Israel took over from the English mandate authority the "Order of Council" according to which all houses in which terrorists had stayed would be blown up. It was claimed in Beirut that by September 1973 about 300 houses had been destroyed on orders from various Israeli commanders. Jewish lawyers had attacked the legality of such retaliation before the state was founded. Blowing up houses is, of course, less radical than shooting hostages but it does affect, in the case of multifamily dwellings especially, a large number of innocents. Moreover, it is futile. It does not take into consideration that terrorists, among the Palestinians in Galilee and in the occupied areas, are intruders. They are unwelcome visitors who usually gain entrance *by force* into both Jewish schools and Palestinian homes. Israeli circles admit that some houses have occasionally been blown up by mistake. Even when individual buildings have been rebuilt at public expense, there is no assurance that all "errors" traced back to false denunciations and conjectures will be corrected. Since in such cases judicial inquiries and decisions are excluded, the action taken by the mili-

tary only serves to intimidate and repress the Palestinians. The horrible acts of terrorism carried out, e.g., in the spring of 1974 and near Tel Aviv in March 1978, were hardly the last. They demonstrate that the counter-terror which Israel has mounted is as ineffective a deterrent as capital punishment in those countries where it still takes place. Since this counter-terror, bombardments, and recently the scorched earth policy applied to refugee settlements in Lebanon, is in effect no less indiscriminate in its selection of victims than the terror itself, and since it is carried out in a proportion of not only "two blows for one" (so Ben Gurion) but more than seven dead Palestinian men, women, and children to one victim from Israel, it cannot even be compared to the barbarity of the death penalty. Why, except in the case of the Nazi criminal Eichmann, Israel asserts its opposition to capital punishment and yet perpetrates (counter-) terrorist strikes and bloody raids, I do not comprehend.

We must ask now whether there is any possible alternative to these measures, which are taken on behalf of Israel's security?

An Israeli general, who was given early retirement, told me that security could not at all be guaranteed by military means. It could rest only on the confidence of the Palestinians in the Jews and on good relationships between both. I am persuaded that he is right. One day, a stronger minority in Israel than only five percent will think as he does. The Yom Kippur War of 1973 demonstrated that Israel, despite its total military, political, and economic control (reaching from Kuneitra on the Golan Heights to the Suez Canal) was as vulnerable and unprotected in its existence as ever. The greater distances which Arab tanks and artillery shells had to overcome gave the responsible Israeli military men a false sense of security. According to statements made by Jewish political commentators and critics, Israel's government and army had apparently learned nothing from General Gamelin's Maginot Line and the futility of a mentality relying on bunkers and guns alone.

All examples mentioned must by no means be understood as proofs of an inherent malice or ineptitude on Israel's side.

Rather they are effects of terrible *temptations* to which Israel, in its hard pressed situation, is exposed and to which—in the opinion of the small minority in Israel mentioned above and of a considerable number of others, especially of young Jews, around the world—Israel has also succumbed. It is understandable that Palestinian and Arab propaganda, as well as many anonymous refugees in the mass camps have reacted to the conditions just described with the sharpest possible condemnation. It is not appropriate for us, however, to join in these expressions of hatred and cries for revenge. Only a person who has been exposed to similar temptations and has resisted them victoriously might be qualified to pass a judgment—and even such a person might prove wise in withholding it. Still, in order to make Israel's distress intelligible not only in its political, military, and financial dimensions but also in its spiritual scope, three additional strong temptations need to be mentioned. There are Jews who realize the danger and look for a way out—with or without the help of Christian friends.

(a) The will to survive can degenerate into a struggle for "survival at any price." But what happens when a surviving son of a Jew no longer wishes to live according to the Jewish Law (in the broad or narrow sense), in other words, as a "Jew"? The book of Deuteronomy ties the gift of the land, together with residence and peace, to obedience to covenant and Law. The prophets combine the promise of a return to the land with a call to repentance, i.e., to a turning back to the order established by the merciful and righteous God. But now the great majority of Jews living in Israel feel only slightly bound by these parts of the Bible. They only want a state like all other states. Religious Jews, however, have a different opinion: a people paying for its survival by submitting completely and fanatically to the ideals and methods of the deities of the heathen would no longer be the Jewish people. Its state might perhaps be a state made up of Jews but it would never be a Jewish state. The name Israel would be a mockery and a derision. It has been Israel's temptation from the beginning to give up its special mission for righteousness and humanity (i.e. its election) and to become a nation "like all the nations." (1 Sam. 8:5)

(b) The love for the land of the fathers can degenerate into an ideology of blood and soil (of the kind found in Leon Uris' *Exodus*) which treats earlier Palestine as a "land without people" and simply subjects it to the alleged superiority of the Jewish "people without land." Gratitude for one's national character and the love for one's country can become a nationalism which corresponds to the mentality of *my country, right or wrong*. Dependence on the protection offered by the army can lead to the triumph of a military mentality which espouses might over right. The danger exists that Israel as a whole will become like those nations which before its time fell victim to a stupid nationalism and a triumphant militarism. There is also the threatening temptation to allow oneself to be misused —even against one's own will and despite one's better judgment—as an advance base of a Western colonialism which still has not died out. I have in mind those completely worked out American plans which envisioned an occupation of Saudi-Arabia and of its oil wells by Israeli troops. The Jewish educator Ernst Simon from Jerusalem voiced the fear in the Bulletin of the Leo Baeck Institute (9: 1966, 21–84), citing Martin Buber, that this development threatened the soul of *all* of Israel far more than had the enforced or voluntary assimilation of Jewish individuals living in the dispersion. What this scholar was recalling and intending as a warning has become severe self-accusation in a statement issued by the World Association of Jewish Students. These students voiced their shame that a nation of oppressed had turned into a nation of oppressors.

(c) It is possible in Israel to close one's eyes to the problem of the Palestinians, as was done by Golda Meir in January 1974, when she made no mention whatever of the Palestinians in her government's statement of policy and at other occasions when she averred, "There are no Palestinians" and "There is no Palestinian problem." It is possible to look upon the Palestinians as actual or potential terrorists because the best known organizations of refugees declared in January 1968 in Cairo that violent conflict constituted their only tactics in the fight for their "rights." Not even at the March 1977 meeting of the Palestinian National Congress at Cairo were the passages of the "Covenant" revised or removed which call for terrorist actions. But to stare only at the paragraphs promoting terror and at the corresponding preparations and actions is one thing; another is the observation of developments within the PLO and the affiliated groups which before and after Arafat's appearance at a U.N. meeting indicate changed tactics. Though not yet prevailing, forces are at work in the National Congress which are convinced that terror has had its day while now the time of political activity and solutions has dawned.

On the other hand, the former Prime Minister of Israel, Yitzhak Rabin, fostered the idea that a dissolution of the refugee camps and a settlement for their inhabitants far from Israel, beyond the Jordan (also the Litani?), would be the "natural" solution to the Palestinian problem. The present Prime Minister, Menachem Begin, with the consent of his government developed in late 1977 a drastic "peace" proposal according to which the Palestinian residents of the West Bank and Gaza Strip choose between Jordanian and Israeli citizenship, receive some elements of political autonomy, but remain under Israeli sovereignty. This "plan" amounts to nothing else than an extension of the present occupation status which Begin likes to call "liberation." However, anyone who believes that one can pacify one's conscience and remove political tensions by proposing measures that forever condemn the Palestinians to an existence in exile or thralldom is harboring an illusion. It is a temptation not only for Israel but also for the Palestinians (as will be shown later) not to want to face facts squarely nor to acknowledge the suffering or the rights of the opposite side. The price for every temptation to which Israel succumbs is paid for, not only by disappointed Jews everywhere whose sensitivity for right and wrong is wide awake, and not only by the hard-pressed Jewish Israelis, but also by the Palestinians living inside and outside of the borders of the state and of the occupied areas. Those condemned to hopelessness will always constitute a threat to those carried by a firm if blind hope.

This does not mean that the Zionist movement which with its intellectual giants, its organizational talent, and its inexhaustible energy, stands behind the State of Israel should be condemned in wholesale fashion or that an "Israel without Zionism" (Uri Avnery) is conceivable. During one of its many, blatantly contradictory phases, Zionism projected, under the influence of high-minded socialists and especially of Martin Buber, e.g., at the XII Zionist Congress in Karlsbad, 1921, a program for the mutual development of Palestine by Jews and Palestinians on the basis of common labor on common land and in opposition to the methods of capitalism and imperialism. In an essay, "Against Unfaithfulness" (*Gegen die Untreue*, 1938, in Martin Buber, *Der Jude und sein Judentum*, Cologne: Joseph Melzer Verlag, 1963, pp. 527 ff.) Buber protested in utter dismay against the fact that this beginning had been displaced by tendencies towards colonialism and pure power politics and thus had been perverted into its very opposite. The *Ichud*, a league for Jewish-Arab rapprochement and cooperation, upheld this view between 1942 and 1948, and some of its former members are still active in the same sense. However, Zionism as a whole has chosen another direction, emphasizing the Jewish monopoly on all vital decisions regarding the state. The present form of Zionism is certainly not the ultimate one and obligates no one to give an unlimited approval to it.

It is, however, necessary, in view especially of the situation, with all of its threat and temptation, in which the State of Israel still continues to find itself, that we affirm its existence unequivocally. At the outbreak of the Yom Kippur War in October 1973, the Swiss writer Friedrich Dürrenmatt declared this bravely and publicly (see *Freiburger Rundbriefe* 25, 1973, nos. 93–96, pp. 56–57): ". . . In many regards, before this new war, the politics of Israel were wrong. . . . Right stands against right in this conflict. . . . The victor was incompetent to win and the defeated incompetent to lose. . . . We need not buy the lies (of the Arabs) because we need their oil . . . With these words I take my stance in support of Israel—out of decency; for the sake of all of us—lest all of us soon become silent." I agree: Israel must not be left standing alone. Our heart goes out to it.

Yet, we now have to turn to the other side in the same way

and with the same perseverance. Calling to mind a minimum
of undisputed facts it is our intention to catch sight of the
self-image of the Palestinians and of their enemy-image.

II. The Palestinians

Even as the conditions and behavior of the State of Israel
since 1948 could only be described and explained by taking its
distress as one's starting point, the Palestinians, too, must be
seen and understood as people in utter distress. As earlier mentioned, Israel's former Prime Minister, Mrs. Golda Meir, has
pontifically declared that "there are no Palestinians,"—a conviction which did not prevent her from having sleepless hours
at night when she thought of the high birthrate among the
Palestinian minority. During her own time, and even more
since she has been replaced by Yitzhak Rabin, and he by Menachem Begin, official statements have shown that she was not
considered infallible. Who are those Palestinians whose very
existence the grand old lady felt constrained to deny?

It is, of course, true that those Jews whose ancestors never
left ancient Palestine or migrated into the land in the course
of the centuries before the end of the British Mandate were also
called "Palestinians." They have every right to contest the
monopolization of the name "Palestinians" by the non-Jewish
inhabitants of the same region. But since the present State of
Israel characterizes itself as Jewish, not as Palestinian, we call
Palestinians those who today claim this name for themselves.

As little as do the Jews in Israel, the Palestinians form a
unified entity. They consist of at least five major groups: (a)
About 450,000 have been Israeli citizens since 1948. (b) Approximately 1,000,000 live in territories occupied by Israel. (c)
The number of those who voluntarily or under compulsion left
the country was probably about 600,000 in 1948. According to
reports from the Palestinian side, today about 1,250,000 live in
camps. Not merely the natural population increase but also
some juggling with registration numbers and food stamps may
account for the difference between the figures. The total of
those exiled in 1948 has almost been matched by the 500,000

Jews who were driven from Arab countries and found shelter in Israel. Israel has not only repatriated 40,000 Palestinians, it also has offered on one occasion to receive back a total of 100,000 "Arabs"—but never more. It is not known how many of the "refugees" would choose to live in Israel, if ever the doors were opened for their return. (d) Other Palestinians are residing temporarily for reasons of work or education, or permanently as immigrants, in other countries of the world, most of them in the Arab states between Basra, Aden, and Casablanca; some also have succeeded in being admitted to the United States. (e) If one were to start from the earlier British conception of the Mandate "Palestine," then the inhabitants of Jordan should also be designated as Palestinian. This, however, would not be agreed to by the east-Jordanian Bedouins who support Hussein's throne.

I stated earlier (p. 51) that many of the Palestinians do not like to be subsumed under the general nomenclature "Arab(s)." Certainly the majority of the Palestinians stem from immigrants who in two waves, after 1882 and 1919, arrived from diverse "Arab" countries. But the term "Arab" can include a cultural element that is distinct from its ethnic and political connotations. "Arabia" means "wilderness," and to live as an Arab can mean to follow, or at least to dream of, a very specific life-style. A person is an Arab, according to one unquenchable school of thought, who masters the art of surviving in the wilderness and prefers unfettered mobility to the tranquillity and possessiveness of settled-down rural and townspeople. Ever since Mohammed in the early days of his religious mission fought, overcame, and converted his sedate relatives at Mecca with the help of the half-Bedouin inhabitants of Medina, a certain wilderness- or Bedouin-romanticism has been present or has periodically resurfaced among Arabs, even in contrast to other trends and capabilities developed among the adherents of Mohammed. At times the wilderness ideology has produced barbaric tactics and frightful results. For instance in Palestine, not only the Jewish settlers arriving in ever increasing numbers after the formation of modern Zionism late in the 19th century, but, long before them, resident farmers and city dwellers under Turkish rule were exposed to attacks from some ancestors of those who today are counted as Palestinians.

The Bedouin garb in which even today Palestinian notables, oil-rich Arab kings, and also PLO chief Yasir Arafat like to be depicted, is a tribute to the priority and superiority still attributed, at least ideologically, to the Bedouin tradition. For this reason, those Palestinians who today are settled more or less comfortably in Israel and the occupied territories are as much afraid of their unsettled brothers as they are resentful of Israel's presence.

Thus, enormous differences exist among the Palestinians as far as self-consciousness, behavior, hopes, and plans are concerned. Not everyone among those holding Israeli citizenship is a potential member of a fifth column; not every refugee is a terrorist; not every emigrant has left his or her homeland solely because of the Jews or the State of Israel. Just as poor and rich, uneducated and educated, weak and strong face one another in Israel, so there is also a wide difference among the Palestinians. There is disparity and contention not only between the individual guerilla groups but also between the notables and the proletariat, between the groups which cooperate with Israel and those which are determined to destroy this state and to replace it by one "modern, democratic state" whose name is to be Palestine. Because they are so split the Palestinians so far have no common address and they are only beginning to find and establish their identity. Who really represents them?

From time immemorial the inhabitants of the land called Palestine by both the Romans and the League of Nations have never been allowed to decide for themselves who would rule over them or speak for them. They were never able to gain experience with a democracy of their own. The experiences the Palestinians did have in the territory which was annexed, occupied, administered, or governed by the Turks, English, Israelis, and Hashemites were always connected with repression, never with full self-determination and democratic responsibility. The Palestinians (at home and in dispersion) do certainly constitute a "population." However, the concept of a Palestinian "people" which is so often used has not yet been clearly defined. Although the United Nations recognizes them as a people and has received Yasir Arafat as their authorized speaker, the Palestinians are certainly not a "nation" in any of the legal and political connotations that this concept has had since the Middle Ages. The diverse backgrounds of the Palestinians prohibit defining them as a tribe. As in the case, for example, of the British or the U.S. citizens, it is only a common history which can weld them together into a nation.

This lack of political and legal order is complicated still further by the Palestinians' inarticulated feeling, moral emotion, and inflamed hope. By speaking of their own "rights" and by working for a state of their own, the Palestinians have begun a process of self-awareness, self-education, and political, social, and military organization that cannot be stopped. They appear to be late-comers and as yet unskilled riders on the waves of the nationalism which has swept Arab and European peoples alike since Napoleon's time. However, since 1948 this has taken a particular form. The old residents of Palestine did not only have common oppressors and common enemies, but also incipient nationalistic movements long before Jews immigrated in masses and "took away their land." The present resurgence of nationalism, since 1948, on the other hand is shaped by the impact of the Jews. What the Jews started eighty years ago when the modern Zionist movement began to take shape now appears to have become the pattern of education and development, of methods chosen, and probably also of success for the Palestinians. They, too, are speaking of their right to their homeland and are dreaming of a truly modern and democratic state with equal rights and freedoms for minorities. Among them, too, religious and ideological motives, catchwords, songs, and orators awaken and arouse concerns and aspirations which not always are concordant with sober and patient political work. Likewise, they not only have detractors, enemies, and persecutors—sometimes in their own ranks—but also, at least during certain periods, helpers in the form of friends around the world who are great in making promises but prove less than reliable when the chips are down. The Palestinians, too, are entering upon unholy alliances. Just as Israel came to depend on America, the Palestinians for their part (especially the then Grand-Mufti of Jerusalem, Hadj Amin-Husseini) once sought to mobilize the protection and help of Hitler. Today, several of their organizations are taking money from the Russians and from oil-producing states. Thus, the Palestinian cause is no less afflicted with contradictions and distress than that of the Israeli.

For years, especially between 1968 and 1973, the use and the glorification of terror tactics have been a reason for the permanent crisis of the Palestinian movement. Palestinian terror is not directed only against Jewish men, women, and children but also against people in their own ranks who are not ready to support the aims and methods of this or that combat organization. It also has found victims among airplane passengers from all nations who had never taken a position in the Israeli-Palestinian conflict. A large number of Palestinians, including in particular some who have been directly affected by Israeli retaliatory measures, however, join the world press in characterizing these acts of terror as "senseless crimes." Indeed, the pain and loss inflicted by raids and bombs, by the murder of children and other innocent victims, and by the willful destruction of property are so grave that there is no way to make light of these tactics. Although, at the Palestinian National Congress meeting in Cairo in March 1977 there might have been a chance to invalidate the passage of the "Palestinian Covenant" which endorsed terror as a political means, this decisive step was not taken.

Although it is impossible to whitewash these actions of the Palestinians, some reflections seem in order lest the Palestinians be considered incomprehensible barbarians.

(1) Historical precedence shows that the use of brutal violence by terrorists, unless they are plainly mad, is provoked by prior use of naked power. Terrorists are people who have been victims of exerted violence, i.e., by a brute military or police corps, by a dictator, by representatives of an economic or cultural system that leaves no hope for freedom and selfhood of

the underdog. Terror endured from the high and mighty is answered by counter-terror. Tired of being used as an anvil, the Palestinians for their part have tried to prove that they, too, can be a hammer. This posture they share with almost all liberation movements wherever these dare to surface.

(2) The Palestinian terrorism moves within the framework of acts carried out by radical Palestinian *and* Jewish groups *against one another* since 1921, when Jewish immigration into Palestine began to increase markedly. Both Palestinians and Jews, the latter chiefly decades ago, have committed wild acts of terror. The fact that Jewish actions were hushed up and that Jews especially would be glad to forget them does not make them any less dreadful than the widely publicized Palestinian acts. I am thinking particularly of the culmination of Jewish terror in the plundering, burning, violation, and murder of the inhabitants of Deir Yassin by the Irgun and the "Stern Group" in April 1948. This crime had a precedent, i.e., in the murder of Jews in Hebron by Palestinians. If Jews do not forget Hebron, how could Palestinians forget Deir Yassin? In the former concentration camp of Bergen-Belsen there is a memorial visited by thousands. Where once stood a flowering Palestinian village there is none, and no retribution of property was made. Thus, Jews *and* Palestinians have to live *after* but also *with* their crimes and losses. "There is here no difference." (Rom. 3:22) On both sides there are murderers and murdered.

(3) In the preparation, evaluation, and acceptance of responsibility for such acts of terrorism, significant differences exist between the Jewish and the Palestinian sides. On both sides there are agencies or quasi-official bureaus which prepare such actions. Irgun and the Stern Group were tolerated and in part armed by the Jewish Agency and the Haganah. Israeli generals have organized counter-terrorist measures such as the assassination of Palestinian leaders in Beirut and the bombing and burning of the "Fatah-land" just as certain political and paramilitary Palestinian organizations have trained, equipped, and sent terrorist groups on their way. When masterstrokes, such as the liberation of hostages at Entebbe, are carried out, one group will speak of ultimate measures provoked

by the opposed group and will praise its own soldiers or agents as national heroes and martyrs while the acts of the opposite side are considered brutal crimes perpetrated by cutthroats. Nevertheless, according to my knowledge, Jews have proved themselves to be prepared, more often than Palestinians and Arabs, to describe crimes as crimes, especially when their own shield is thereby dirtied and their own conscience is burned. I mention Martin Buber once more, and also the moral condemnation of the Irgun and the Stern Group after Deir Yassin by a Jewish court of law and by the Jewish Agency. Why did the Palestinian organizations in the camps and the Arab governments not react with sharp condemnation to Munich, Maalot, Kiryat Shemona and similar slaughters? Why, on the contrary, are additional terrorist ventures prepared even though thoughtful Palestinians inside and outside of the refugee camps (including people from Arafat's staff) are conscious of the devastating effect that brutal murders have on Israel, worldwide Judaism, and world opinion? I have no answer to this question. Apparently, what strikes us Western people as inhuman, unrealistic, politically counter-productive and, therefore, stupid is evaluated quite differently in Arab quarters —at least among those who still cling to the earlier mentioned Bedouin traditions. In most cases, Bedouins do not wage war in order to conquer land—nomads do not feel protected nor fettered by boundaries—but to repel oppressors or to intimidate those who despise them. When the enemy is too strong, the tactics of sham-retreats and roundabout surprise attacks are employed for dealing an impressive blow. Even when they are the weaker party, the erection of a sign showing "we are still here" saves the honor and makes the dash worthwhile. While we in the Christianized West may have different ideas about methods and purposes of warfare, the millions slaughtered by our armies demonstrate that we have no reason to feel morally superior.

Israel must, of course, listen to the cries of its own citizens who have been victims of terrorists; it has enough of its own tears to dry. Nonetheless one must ask whether the deafness of the government and parliament along with the counter-terror of the Israeli armed forces, do not pour oil on the fire? Do they not, therefore, also share responsibility for the terrible "method of communication" used by desperate Palestinian extremists?

(4) In Rollo May's book, *Power and Innocence: A Search for the Sources of Violence* (N.Y. : Norton, 1972), terror is described as the final means for communicating total frustration to others—as a universal human language which is spoken only when a rational method of communication no longer exists. This description is hardly valid for the behavior of governmental agencies, including the military. However, it does make sense with respect to the human condition in which the Palestinians in the refugee camps and the occupied territories find themselves today. Activists resort to terror because they have reason to be afraid that the world could or would want to forget them. Thus it is possible to understand terror as the cry of distress. It is obvious that peaceful citizens are deeply shocked by such outcries.

(5) The number, not the cruelty and the catastrophic results of the terror-strikes have decreased in the last few years. The large scale Palestinian action which ended at Entebbe was organized by George Habash's Popular Front for the Liberation of Palestine, which is at the point of rebellion against Arafat's leadership of the PLO. The main reasons for the change in PLO tactics (before the Tel Aviv attack in March 1978) were the following: the effect of Israeli counter-measures; the growing recognition in Palestinian quarters of the counter-productive impact on public opinion; the political success gained by Yasir Arafat's appearance before the U.N.; the sham-victory gained for the Palestinian cause when on Nov. 10, 1975 a majority of the U.N. made the absurd declaration that Zionism is racism; the engagement and decimation of the Palestinian guerillas in the Lebanese civil war, especially in the fall of Camp Tel Zaatar. Although there are still strong elements among the Palestinians in exile that call for a continuation and increase of terrorism, Yasir Arafat and a growing number of his Pales-

tinian and Arab supporters might still come to the insight that
political means will lead eventually to better results. Obviously the decisive step to be taken by the National Congress
of the Palestinians would be to follow the example first set by
Egypt on milestone 101 between Suez and Cairo, then by un-
counted secret and public agreements with the U.S. and Israel, finally by Sadat. This way the existence of Israel would
be recognized *de facto*. If Israel at the same time recognized
at least the PLO as a *de facto* representation of the Palestinians, preferring diplomatic talks to open military action, a decisive step toward the abandonment of terror-tactics on both
sides would be made. Perhaps, Yasir Arafat will still change
from a guerilla leader to a politician. Consequently he has to
fight radical opposition in his own ranks as intensively as the
overwhelming pressures induced from outside. If ever Arafat
or his skillful spokesman on foreign affairs, Farouk Kad-
doumi, should fall victim to assassination, Israel will probably
regret that it has refused to encourage the alternatives to terrorism for which the PLO seemed to be ready. But despite
rumors about occasional secret contacts, overtures made by
the moderate PLO wing for initiating direct conversations
have been rebuffed by a discouraging sign of Israel's increasing intransigence.

All that so far has been said about terrorism should suffice
to show that the simplistic (Israeli) equation, "Palestinians are
terrorists," is untenable. However, while the same patriotic
passion is found among Israelis and Palestinians, and while the
balance of violence is about even, there is still a very unequal
distribution of actual power. Compared with Israel, the Palestinian liberation movement has been weaker in every respect
—even before its strongholds were routed in the spring of 1978.

(a) Instead of an effective state the Palestinians have com-
peting political and paramilitary organizations. To this day not
only Israel but also the United States and other Western countries refuse to recognize them. The reception of Yasir Arafat in
the U.N. and several U.N. majority votes condemning or ma-
ligning Israel were theatrical éclats, indeed, but they did not

really change the situation of the outcast and outlaw. Both the Arab states and the Russians, who on occasion seem to speak for them, are first of all concerned with their own advantage. The Palestinians have not yet been able to spell out their oft-mentioned "rights." I have received only evasive answers when I asked about the contents of a potential constitution for the modern, democratic state being dreamed of. A formulation of the claimed or hoped for rights would necessarily have to include more than "interests" and "aspirations." It would have to recognize obligations with respect to the legal equality of Jews and Palestinians as well as guarantees for the security needs of others. Above all, it would have to include the recognition of the State of Israel. In summary, the Palestinians have made even less progress on the road to legal equality than Israel.

(b) Even though Israel's financial situation and the tax burden of its citizens are dreadful, most Palestinians, as well as their organizations, are even poorer. Although third world powers may sympathize with them, they are not able to deliver regularly to them the kind of resources which worldwide Judaism supplies to Israel. The subsidies coming from the oil countries are irregular or are kept barely sufficient because, among other things, of the socialistic if not revolutionary orientation of the majority of the refugee organizations.

(c) Israel's military forces, its police, and administration are better equipped and more successful in the control of the Palestinians than the British ever were in the mandated territory. The Palestinians have suffered enormous losses in human life, in military strength, and in worldwide respect. Their loss of power was multiplied by the invasion of Israel into southern Lebanon.

(d) Jewish mass media understood very well, in times of crisis and war, how to extend the will to resist and the strength to hold out even to the most remote kibbutz. They also mobilized world opinion for Israel. During the same periods, however, Arab radio stations spread fictional situation reports and impossible promises, calling on the Palestinians to flee. For a

great number of Palestinians this propaganda was the main
reason for leaving their country and possessions. Also, by the
use of atrocious threats against the Jews, the Arab radio stations succeeded in mobilizing the opinion of the whole Western
world against the Arabs and Palestinians. The result was a
growing self-confidence among the Jews in the mandated territory—and later on in Israel. On the other hand, among the
Palestinians, self-confidence was increasingly shaken and ever
stronger doubts arose about those Arab states that pretended
to act as "friends" and "relatives." While Arab self-consciousness and pride flared up during and after the Yom Kippur War,
the Palestinians had little reason to boast because the contribution of their military organizations to the early victories of
Israel's enemies was less than conspicuous; the armies of Egypt
had borne the brunt.

(e) In 1972 Cecil Hourani, in the Beirut paper *El Nahar*
under the title "The Moment of Truth" called on the Arab
powers finally to become clearheaded and to carry on a policy
of realism. This Arab voice was still like the peep of a lonely
bird. Only in the last few years has there been any evidence of
cooperation: first, Anwar as-Sadat of Egypt began to cooperate
with a search for peace as promoted by Henry Kissinger and of
late by Cyrus Vance; then, Hafez el Assad's Syria, by its intervention in the Lebanese civil war, radically turned its back on
the former policies of mere big words. Finally King Hussein of
Jordan has—at times in self-contradictory utterances for or
against Palestinian claims—remained eager and open for a
termination of the state of war.

Before this turn, a foolish misjudgment of their relative
strength had led the Arab states, for example, to reject the
U.N.'s decision of 1947 on the partition of Palestine. This was
followed by a call for the withdrawal of U.N. troops and the
blockade of the seaways and thus provided the occasion for the
Six-Day War of 1967.

(f) The last problem of the Palestinians to be mentioned
stems less from attributes and attitudes of their own than from
the limited capacity of Westerners to understand the special
situation, mentality, and way of life that characterize near-

Eastern peoples. To Western Christians, Arabs and Palestinians are much more of a riddle than the western and eastern-European Jews who at present are dominant in the State of Israel. The confidence in the promised Messiah, the common part of the Bible, the road traveled together during almost 2000 years have left traces. Willingly or not, Western Jews and Christians have been welded together. Although the common history is marked by Jewish blood and tears shed as a result of the churches' anti-Judaistic attitude, it is still possible to say that basically both Jews and Christians view the same things as an evil, a temptation, a desirable goal, or a joy. With Arab people there are points of contact which certainly prohibit the notion that the Moslems are "pagans." The Koran (which has coined all that is called Arab) has endorsed doctrinal and ethical elements of the Bible. Also, the names of Baghdad and Cordoba recall sites and periods of flourishing Arab culture to which Western science and art are deeply indebted. Moslem Arabs may like to harken back to Bedouin wilderness origins and patterns—yet, their contributions to the life of settled populations are enormous. Regrettably, except for some scholars, missionaries, and travelers, we Western people know so little of Islam and *"arabité,"* its developments, tensions, and potentials, that we cannot yet converse with its representatives in the same brotherly way as with Jews. That inexplicable and inexcusable psychological block which is often felt between Christians and Jews, even when they fight innate prejudices, is still more potent in the relations between Christians and Moslems, Westerners and Arabs. Eventually, the churches in the chiefly Moslem countries of Asia and Africa, might play an important role in bridging the as yet existing chasm. If, for example, the Coptic and the Maronite Churches were willing to shoulder this task, they would not only have to transmit the anti-Zionist grievances of their environment to the West, they might also—just as the Western churches are beginning to do —call their own members to repentance for the absence of concern for the Jewish people if not for crimes committed against them. Any judgment passed in the name of God cannot be true except it "begins with the household of God," that is, except Christians subject themselves to it first.

We close this section by discussing (1) the special problems posed by one "Arabic" state, Lebanon; and (2) the specific political aspirations held by organized Palestinian refugees.

1. We ask first of all why the Palestinian question has not been resolved long ago by the peaceful settlement and naturalization of those Palestinians who are presently living as so-called "refugees" outside of Israel and West Jordan. The United Nations prevents the starvation of about 1,250,000 Palestinians (including an unknown number of people who joined them voluntarily) who live in camps by spending thirty-five cents (American valuation) per day and per person for food, shelter, education, and hygiene. The outward living conditions in the tent and cabin camps are equal to those of a very poor Arab village where men and women lack regular work and means for economic progress. Only Palestinians with extraordinary drive, skill, and luck have been able to dodge the Arab host-countries' laws prohibiting naturalization and employment and to work their way up. Others have emigrated.

The situation of Lebanon before the civil war may explain why the camps have not been closed long ago. Lebanon had about 2,800,000 inhabitants including the 600,000 resident Syrians and the 350,000 refugees. According to the latest census, one-half (more accurately six-elevenths) of the citizens of Lebanon were Christian, while two-thirds of the remainder were Sunnite and one-third Shiite Moslems. Following the establishment of the state of Lebanon an internal agreement of the political forces stated in 1943 that the country's president would be a Christian, the prime minister a Sunnite, his deputy a Shiite, and that in the parliament, in the administration, in the military, in the postal service, in the police a similar troika would have control of the direction of countryside and city. Though the state constitution provided regular repetition of the census and of elections, the three ruling groups agreed after the first period—during which wave after wave of Palestinian refugees had arrived—not to allow the existing equilibrium to be upset by a new census and general elections. Thus the ruling groups remained in power—at the expense not only of the growing Moslem majority but also of the refugees, who thus were condemned to decades of inactivity and hopelessness.

Already before the civil war the ire of the refugees and the fear of the ruling classes led to severe clashes. Opinions are divided as to which side provoked the other in certain cases, when, under the leadership of the liberation movements which administered the camps, Palestinians made armed forays in and outside Lebanon, and Lebanese armed forces bombarded from the air or by artillery the camps for hours or days until another oral armistice created a longer or shorter pause in the fighting. In one camp in Beirut, for example, around 300 refugees were killed in this manner by Lebanese armed forces during April 1973. The problems thus persist. Lebanon's army and police, whose number has been variously placed at 3,500 or at 15,000, are not willing, despite their grandiose war ministry and their superior armament, simply to liquidate the refugees. They could not drive them out because no neighboring country was willing to take them. The disunity between its Christian and Moslem parts made it too weak to control the activity of terrorists on its side of the common border with Israel.

Before the civil war, Lebanon had behaved towards the Palestinians like an established rich man towards a poor person who has no rights. One can, in fact, characterize the Palestinian refugees, with or without recourse to Marx, as poor people who have been deprived of their rights. They seem to be so worthless that they are not even exploited economically. All Arab host countries have, moreover, their own unemployed. Nevertheless, the Sagorsk Declaration of the All-Christian Peace Conference (1967) is in error when it regards all Arabs as exploited poor. Capitalism in its pure form, even behind the facade of middle-class or semi-socialist governments, does not just exist in the United States and in Israel but also among the oil-producing states and in Lebanon, Jordan, and Egypt as well. This is the reason that the refugees have thus far not found real friends anywhere, not even in Russia. They are used—and sacrificed—like pawns in the national and international games of chess. Their poverty is among the reasons for their own internal disunity and their unwise tactics.

In the Lebanese civil war the fires which erupted had been smoldering ever since the Lebanese Constitution was invalidated by the internal agreement of those controlling the state in 1943. Just as in the case of Ireland, roots of the civil war did not lie merely in religious conflicts. Much more important in Lebanon are tensions and clashes, also ever-changing unholy alliances between interest groups such as the following: the almost feudal ruling circles and the upper bourgeoisie with their international business connections and their profits from huge capitals invested by oil-producing states; the upcoming conservative Christian middle class (represented by the Phalange) and, slightly more to the left, its Moslem counterpart; the mostly Arab and partly Marxist urban and rural proletariat (whose spokesman was the radical Gamal Jumblatt); the Palestinians in their camps, and the Palestinian units that form part of the Syrian army. The merciless battles fought, the massacres, as well as the destruction of property were the well known results—until the open intervention of regular Syrian troops stopped the indiscriminate bloodshed and devastation. Yet, the same groups may still be waiting for the next round.

Among the strange effects of the Lebanese civil war was the humanitarian and military cooperation between Israel and the Phalange (allegedly Christian), signaled by the opening of the once rigidly closed northern frontier of Galilee and its transmutation into a so-called "good fence." The humanitarian measures taken by Israel, for example, the hospitalization of wounded and the feeding or employment of hungry people from the southern regions of Lebanon, may well indicate the beginning of a new chapter in Israeli relations to both Christians and Arabs. Charity, however, is hardly Israel's only motive. The logistic, artillery, tank, and air support given to the Phalange also serves security interests of Israel: the reformation of Palestinian military strength is to be prevented, and Syrian troops are to be held afar. Lebanese patriots ventilate the fear that the water shortage of Israel might induce Israel eventually to secure for itself access to the waters of the upper Litani and Orontes rivers. At present it is impossible to verify this apprehension.

Another result of the civil war is the reinforced negative attitude of the Israeli majority against the idea of a Palestinian state. This concerns not only the outspoken purpose of the "Palestinian Covenant," which is to replace the Jewish state including the occupied territories and, perhaps, additional territories (Jordanian, Syrian, and Lebanese ?) with a modern democratic State of Palestine. It also pertains to the diverse intimations regarding a future Palestinian mini-state consisting of the West Bank and the Gaza Strip. It is argued in Israel that the Lebanese civil war has demonstrated how suicidal it is for ethnic and religious minorities to live among an Arab majority. Since peaceful coexistence did not work in Lebanon, so Jewish voices conclude, it would not succeed in any larger or smaller Palestinian state either.

The Jews' need for security in Israel, and their right to attain it, are unquestionable. Indeed, they have had to face easily kindled emotions, rash and volatile decisions, unpredictable acts, not to speak of the expulsion of Jews and the cruel treatment of those prevented from emigration from near-eastern Arab states. It is, however, less than convincing when the blame for the Lebanese chaos is put alone or primarily on the Palestinians and when it is presumed that a display of their special intentions is to be seen in the graveyards and ruins of Beirut and many a Lebanese town and village. In fact, the Palestinians so far have had hardly any chance to show in Lebanon or elsewhere what they would contribute to the existence of a democratic state. There are, of course, "Palestinians" in the Jordanian government and parliament; a few of them form their own parties or are members of other (mostly leftist) parties in the Knesset. Although their role in both the monarchic state of Jordan and the republic of Israel resembles that of second-class citizens, there are enough competent, sober, moderate people among them to justify the expectation that they can pave a way towards democratic autonomy. If only Israel were wise enough to permit them their own political organizations! In any case, the Lebanese war should not be used as an excuse to deny forever to the exiled Palestinians the capability for peaceful organization and, eventually, for the establishment of their own state. When President Jimmy Carter, who certainly is a friend of Israel, spoke in March 1977 of a "national home" for the Palestinians he may have intentionally alluded to the Balfour Declaration of 1917—the first official political step toward the formation of the later State of Israel.

2. We ask further: in spite of their troubles from which there seems to be no way out, what goal do the Palestinians have? What hopes do they have in life?

In and outside of the camps one can find desperate people who are lost in daydreams and have no hopes at all. There are people who are expecting an improvement in the lot of the Palestinians only two generations from now through some kind of new constellation of the world's powers. Others again are doing everything to obtain entry into one of the countries across the sea and to find, along with their new life, a new nationality. Meanwhile the more or less militant groups are collecting volunteers and inducing hesitaters to join in their military preparations.

Among the Palestinians within the borders of Israel and in the occupied territories there are on the one hand those who are well situated and earn good money. They seem prepared to acquiesce in the present conditions. On the other hand, there are masses who are scarcely aware of what they are lacking, what they have lost, or what they might achieve. There have been strict controls, relentless expulsions, preventive detentions, and scandalous treatment of those who have been arrested. These have contributed to the fact that among the old notables, e.g., the mayors of the major cities, as well as the owners of businesses and property, the workers on the land and in industry, the students, and the proletariat of the occupied territories a *prise de conscience* has not occurred. In other words, a development of socio-political or national consciousness through discussions, demonstrations, meetings, new parties, newspapers, and other publications has not taken place. Still, it is unlikely that the inhabitants of West Jordan and of the Gaza Strip will indefinitely waive the right to make their own decisions and to have them respected. They will not allow that their future be determined solely by the PLO. Israel is playing into the hands of people more radical than Arafat as long as it continues to maintain its present attitude. Though against its own will, Israel is nevertheless the father of the present radical Palestinian nationalism.

The establishment of a West-Jordanian university, which would eventually be Moslem and independent of the State of Israel would have been a necessary first step towards the discovery and formation of a cultural and social Palestinian identity. One needs only to think of the function of the Hebrew University on behalf of Judaism and the State of Israel. But up to this time it has not been possible to carry through with plans for a Palestinian university. There is an excellent Palestinian college, Bir Zeit, in the occupied territory of the West Bank. But because of some student demonstrations its distinguished head, Hanna Nazir, was expelled from the land, and the quality of the school suffers correspondingly. A future nation's consciousness of its history and responsibility is inconceivable without the intelligentsia. However, as a result of political reasons and a *de facto* admissions quota, the potential Palestinian intelligentsia has very limited chances to enter Israeli institutions of higher learning. It is true that those young people from the refugee camps or the occupied territories who are attending the universities of Beirut, Damascus, Amman, or Cairo provide proof that a Palestinian is by no means condemned, because of his or her past, to remain forever and all time a child of the desert, a farmer with a wooden plow or a muzzled subject. More than 1,300 years of Arab culture have left astonishing traces among them. But the Palestinian students are so isolated, they have so little hope for future employment, their demand for justice and freedom is so embarrassing to their hosts that many —especially the Christians among them—would rather die as freedom fighters than live in a way that is devoid of meaning and hope.

When in the fall of 1973 I visited Palestinian camps in Lebanon, and when I met with Arafat and with high-ranking members of the PLO leadership, I asked for concrete ideas and plans regarding the political course to be taken in the near future. What I learned then has in the meantime been confirmed by the more or less public discussions—though not yet by binding resolutions—of the Palestinian National Congress meeting at Cairo in June 1974 and March 1977. Omitting the propaganda to which we are all exposed, the following information appears to be worth mentioning:

(a) A reconsideration of the situation is under way. It is occurring inside the responsible leadership of the El Fatah with Yasir Arafat at its head, possibly also in the "Democratic Popular Front" under the leadership of the socialist ideologue, Nayef Hawatmeh, and least of all in the case of George Habash and his "Popular Front for the Liberation of Palestine" (PFLP). Also, there is as yet no evidence that within the "Black September" group a rethinking is taking place. Large groups of Palestinians have demonstrated their willingness to recognize Israel and its 3,000,000 present inhabitants as a state. Certainly there has grown within the PLO (the delegates of the united resistance forces) a readiness to be satisfied, for the time being, with the formation of an independent mini-state of Palestine consisting of the occupied West Jordan territories and the Gaza Strip. The limited goal indicates the beginning of a turn from totalitarian demands and from a belief in a final military solution. Here is the onset of political thinking. Arafat does not yet speak publicly of this change of position—probably because of his fear that a radical wing of the El Fatah might brand him as a traitor and go over to the PFLP or to even more revolutionary groups. Even so, there is the threat of a dissolution of the PLO by a splitting away from it of all radical groups. Unfortunately, however, official circles in Israel, continue to insist that all persons organized for liberation are to be considered and treated as terrorists. Similarly, many of the terrorists see the real intentions of Israel embodied only in the radical position taken by the right-wing group, "Likud." Its former spokesman, Menachem Begin was in 1948 the commander of the Irgun and is today Prime Minister. When will people on both sides learn to make distinctions among people and to take changes of opinion seriously so that finally they might enter upon realistic negotiations?

(b) For a long time after the June War of 1967 the Palestinians in the camps, at the West Bank, and in the Gaza Strip, set no hope upon King Hussein. Too vivid was the impact of the "Black September" of 1970, during which this Hashemite ruler, in order to retain his hold on the reins of power, ordered bombing raids, which killed some 10,000–20,000 of their people. Not even Hussein's claim to be an offspring of Mohammed's family made the Moslem majority among them wish and work for a return of the occupied territories to the State of Jordan. It is as yet uncertain whether the rebirth of the monarchist sympathies among anti-socialist Palestinians and the recent rapprochement (and meeting) between Arafat and the king will not force the PLO to give up its claim to be the exclusive representative of the Palestinians. The Palestinians to whom I spoke expected that a complete or partial return of the West Bank to Jordanian control would result not in a liberation deserving of that name but only in their being shackled for an indefinite time to a feudal rule which in the end would fall and disappear.

Ever since King Farouk was replaced by President Nasser, first Egypt and then a succession of Arab states ranging from Tunisia to Iraq and the Sudan, have experimented with a type of democracy in which the head of state is at the same time *primus inter pares* in a national governing council (where he may be voted down) and a charismatic leader of the masses who derives his rights from the people's applause. "Consensus Democracy" may be a fitting designation of this constitutional idiosyncrasy. While Arafat's relation to the PLO leadership and to the Palestinian people in the camps very much resembles this Arab form of democracy, Hussein is a monarch who owes his position not to a consensus but originally to Great Britain and increasingly to the United States. In addition, his throne reposes upon the support of his own (east-Jordanian) Bedouins whose interests often conflict with those of the West Bank Bedouins and the settled Palestinians on both sides of the river. It is inconceivable that King Hussein should have a vital interest in the resettlement of refugees in West Jordan. Perhaps this is the real reason why Israel is still flirting with him. In Israel's official circles a potential West Bank state has been described as a pan-Arab or Russian spearhead aimed at Israel.

(c) The Palestinian concepts of the future constitution and policy of the hoped for mini-state are still extremely vague— except in two respects. (1) This state should be a modern democracy. (2) This state does not want to tie itself in terms of its foreign policy to one of the great power blocks, neither does it want to be dependent upon oil money nor become only a reservoir of cheap labor for Israel.

Some of Arafat's assistants told me of their hope that the necessarily close economic relations between the mini-state, Jordan, and Israel might lead after some years to a federation, first with Israel and later with other neighboring states. It was their opinion that, following the model of Switzerland or of Yugoslavia, an Israeli-Palestinian-Jordanian federal state might be formed as the heart of a near-eastern neutral block. In Israel the idea of a binational state is as old as Yehuda Magnes and Martin Buber. It almost seems to have died with them under the pressure of the experiences following 1948. The transitional goal of a loose federation of states has also been propagated for years by the Jewish World Congress under the leadership of Nahum Goldmann and by prominent academic persons and journalists in Israel. The establishment of a small state consisting of the West Bank and the Gaza Strip might at least be a step on the steep path towards that objective.

A number of Palestinians perceive, in any case, that the development of a constitution will involve a period of one or two years. During this period troops of the United Nations would exert military control over the new nation (in order to allay Israeli fears and to exclude unwanted interventions), while representatives of the refugees and their organizations, of the notables and landowners, of businessmen and the petty bourgeoisie, and also of the workers and students together would work out a constitution in which the concerns of the returning exiles and of those who remained in the land would be adjusted to one another in the best possible way. In this manner the identity and address of a Palestinian nation might be established.

The idea of such a state and the corresponding abandonment of territory held since the Six-Day War finds widespread opposition in Israel. Not only the radical Prime Minister Menachem Begin, but equally his predecessor Yitzhak Rabin who was counted as a moderate and was forced to resign in Spring 1977 because of a non-political reason, have absolutely refused to recognize the PLO and to discuss the idea of a mini-state or any homeland for the Palestinians. Still, it remains to be seen whether the "hawkish" successor to Rabin can achieve what a Nixon and a de Gaulle as exponents of rightist circles did when they recognized Red China and the independence of Algiers respectively. Begin (or after his foreseeable failure, a potentially less radical successor) might eventually recognize the PLO as a (among several others) Palestinian discussion partner and give his consent to the formation of a small Palestinian state. This state could be founded only under conditions compatible with Israeli security needs. At the same time, without the simultaneous recognition of the State of Israel by the PLO and other Palestinian representatives such a way to peace is not viable.

We turn now to a consideration of Christian responsibility in the conflict and distress of the two peoples.

III. The Responsibility of Christians

We have thus far placed side by side the unalterable facts and glowing hopes, many horrible crimes, and a few promising beginnings. Nevertheless, one cannot simply paint in black and white. Under no circumstances are we simply to speak of people as good or bad. The Near East conflict is not a fairy tale, a myth, or a western movie which thrives on such contrasts. One-sided partisanship, in the sense of a decision by the churches for unconditional support of present-day Zionism or of the present-day opponents of Israel, is no contribution to peace but enlarges the conflagration. This is also true of decisions which are made when information is lacking about "the other side," or as a result of historically conditioned prejudices, or on the basis of ideological analyses of history, or simply because of sheer stubbornness.

It should have become clear that in the conflict between Israel and the Palestinians "right stands against right"— which is a formulation coming originally from a Jew in Israel —but also that wrong stands against wrong, need against need, and that a blind self-idealization and bedeviling of one's opponent are to be found on both sides. The more or less latent permanent condition of war brings out not the best but the worst in both partners.

Should we then speak of the situation as tragedy? In the pursuit of high goals, criminal means are employed on both sides and great guilt is piled up. Yet, tragedy, in a classic sense, presupposes polytheism. Because various gods stand against each other in unsolvable conflict, human beings must endure the conflict and can at best only perish heroically in it. Persons are in that case actors, spectators, and victims of the existing tensions. The appeal to gods and traditions demanding one's commitment—whether in this instance to the God who promised the land and Zion to Israel, or to Allah who has a sanctuary in Jerusalem and on occasion commanded that Jews and Christians be tolerated—may give the combatants on both sides a "good conscience." Still, such a good conscience, as experience shows, is more likely to come out in favor of a contest for peace through victory than of reconciliation.

But what if only One is truly God and what if this God is not only distinct from an ideological construction but is also a scathing critic and the only alternative to a subjugation of human beings to ideologies? The faith and the confession of Jews, Moslems, and Christians must not be understood as three parallel monotheistic systems. True adherents of these "religions" do not insult one another as heathens but believe in the uniqueness, unity, and identity of the one God, who is indeed worshiped by them in very different ways. For this reason the escape into a mythological—dualistic, hence hopeless, world view is open to none of them.

What this means for all those concerned Jews and Christians who ask for orientation and encouragement is to be discussed now. (a) About Hegel it has been said that he had to settle the world's great conflict in his own soul, with the result that he became a passionate fighter on both sides. This should also be true of us. (b) A leading American rabbi said to me, "You Christians should be neither Zionists nor blind partisans of the Arabs. But bring the Arabs and us to the same table." This is most difficult and leads to disappointing experiences—but it expresses a felt need and a fostered hope that must not be bypassed. (c) It cannot be our task, in our hearts or in the company of Jews and/or Arabs, to play the part of a judge in order to vindicate one or the other. We must, however, speak of the one God in whose government faithfulness to the people of Israel, compassion for widows and orphans and unfortunates from all peoples, as well as the strength and will to establish justice where injustice reigns, do not stand in tension or contradiction to one another but are held together by a single love. This love will recognize Israel's fears and claims for security and prove understanding of grave mistakes made in its pursuit. Since this love is indivisible it will seek peace also for those Palestinians who now are oppressed, exiled, dispersed and, in part, misguided by demagogues and radicals. In any case, it will do more than call for charitable relief, deplore unrealistic and intransigent politics, and condemn terror actions. It will stand up for the needs and hopes of Israel among those who ask for the rights of the Palestinian people, and vice versa. Such love is not only a matter of faith but also a criterion of faith; where it becomes reality it demonstrates that neither love nor faith are impracticable dreams on the field of politics. Three things have to be pointed out in this context:

(1) To believe in God, in view of the present situation, means to hold on to and to build upon the certainty that reconciliation and peace really do exist, even in situations where there is apparently no way out. The establishment and proclamation of reconciliation and peace (2 Cor. 5:18–20; Eph. 2: 11–18) are, as a result of the coming of Jesus Christ and the work of the Holy Spirit, reality and not wishful dreaming or

utopia—even though what we are now seeing with our own eyes may utterly contradict them. The divine justice made known to us is called "justification of the sinner," whether the sinner be of Jewish or non-Jewish origins. As a professor of New Testament I feel myself obligated to more than expositions about the historical and literary origin of and the parallels to such statements. I have to ask for their content, the history of their influence, and finally, the demands they make of us. The apostles *have* not only spoken, they still speak to us even today through the Bible. "Today if you hear his voice harden not your hearts!" (Ps. 95:7–8) We know that love and reconciliation alone are the forces which can set right what is wrong and can form the basis for just demands and measures.

It looked like progress when, in 1966 at Canterbury and in 1974 at Cartigny and Bad Saarow, boards of the World Council of Churches set the rights of the Palestinians over against the rights of Israel. But the price which had to be paid for this was that in Israel people are now talking of a defection of the World Council of Churches and of individual Western Christians to the "Arabs." Nevertheless, among Christians of the West there has been much too little, not too much, rethinking. For the reality and message of love and reconciliation have thus far still not been discussed and proclaimed with the same intensity as the "rights" of this or that side—or of both sides. In my opinion the special responsibility of Christians consists today not in drawing up or repeating various theses on natural, national, or general human rights but solely and alone in taking the great and small steps which testify to, lead to, and promote reconciliation.

The chief event of the Cartigny Conference of January 1974 was not the declaration which was drawn up there concerning the respective rights and mutual legal obligations of the Israelis and the Palestinians. A hundred times more important is the fact that one evening two approximately thirty-year old persons, one a radical Jewess of French nationality, the other an equally enthusiastic representative of the Palestinian Liberation Front, could sit at the same table and talk to each other as human beings, person to person, even about their disagreements. The possibility of a reconciliation of the differences seemed to be moving into sight, although still not near enough to be grasped. Malicious people speak of the Massada-, Auschwitz-, Deir Yassin-, or September-complex among present-day authoritative Israeli and Palestinian leaders. They forget that we all suffer from complexes. Nevertheless, the need to repent for grave mistakes and crimes and the hope for a fundamentally new beginning in attitude and behavior on both sides remain valid.

(2) To believe in God means, moreover, to believe in the reality and possibility of a new human being. It is clear that without a change in human hearts no reconciliation and no lasting peace can come to pass. Israelis who are favorably inclined towards the Arabs still think today that all would be well if only the good intentions of the Jews could be carried out and if only the outstretched Jewish hand would finally be grasped by the Palestinians. Likewise many Palestinians still think that they themselves could and would—once they had achieved control—properly define and protect the legitimate interests of the Jewish residents and immigrants in the State of Israel. Thus two imperialistic claims stand over against one another. Israel promises the Palestinians that it will protect them by devouring them. The same kind of protection the Palestinians, for their part, promise the Israelis.

But the manner and way in which, according to Paul, Jews and non-Jews become reconciled to one another consist therein that out of *both* there is made a new human being, that all take off the old human nature and put on the new one (Eph. 2:15; 4:22–24). This seems to me to be thought and said perfectly. It concerns the whole human being and, therefore, deals with one's religion as well as with one's politics and one's everyday behavior. The content of the gospel is the realistic politics of God who knows how justice is created. Israelis and Palestinians, and also we ourselves, will conform to this realistic politics only when each person begins the transformation personally.

The same thing can also be stated by using psychological

concepts. The present-day Jewish Israeli receives a substantial part of his or her identity not only through his or her relationship to fellow Jews but also through the relationship to Palestinians. Similarly, the discovery and development of the identity of the Palestinians is determined substantially by their Zionist opposites. If each partner needs the other in order to be self-actualized then hatred of the other means self-destruction, but community with the other means to build oneself up. The commandment, "Love your neighbor as yourself," hardly appeals to self-love as the basis for love of one's neighbor. It does proclaim, however, that only in a social relationship with another human being (whether lovable, embarrassing, or hostile) can a person find, maintain, and retain one's own self.

If Christians were to assign a subordinate rank to love and reconciliation in their anthropology, sociology, psychology and politics, they would thereby prove that they despise God's promise and command that human identity, authenticity, and dignity are found through renewal.

Karl Marx with his belief in the humanizing of human beings would then precede them into the Kingdom of Heaven. In my opinion neither the Jews in Israel nor the Palestinians have been able thus far to discover and achieve their identity fully because they have tried to do so against one another, rather than with one another. So both still boast of their democratic aims while still treating one another as imperialists and terrorists, respectively. Both need one another for security—both as separate entities and as one entity. We can help them to get to know, to acknowledge, and to accept one another. Perhaps we can do that best by first learning to respect and accept the misery and the promise—and above all the human beings—on both sides.

(3) To believe in God means finally to speak here and to be silent there and keep oneself from falling victim to either the enticements or the threats of one or the other partner in the conflict. We all stand on Israel's side in abhorring the barbarous attacks made by Palestinian terrorists. At the same time, the Israeli counter-terror, exerted especially between 1967 and 1973, and in south Lebanon in 1978, was no less abhorrent: for

the great majority of those killed and wounded by Israeli bombs and raids were innocent victims, and those who were guilty of their death are our brothers. Under these circumstances would one-sided protests, such as Jewish friends expect from Christians, be appropriate? We tremble when Israel is attacked militarily as it was in 1973 when Arab nations sought revenge for their defeat in 1967. But we have to admit that a false sense of security and the unwillingness of Israel under the leadership of Golda Meir to make proposals and offer concessions contributed to the outbreak of the Yom Kippur War. Can we be expected to cry out on the one hand and to be silent on the other? When in October 1973 prominent Jewish Israelis called upon the World Council of Churches to make a loud pro-Israeli declaration, several church leaders in Arab countries demanded an opposite public reaction: each group hoped that their war would be declared just and holy. However, since during the medieval crusades Christians themselves had slaughtered thousands of Jews and Arabs, it would have ill befitted them to encourage a further identification of any such war with God's cause.

Although we also suffer when deeds of violence are committed and innocent blood is shed, we are not obligated to be a mouthpiece of public reaction and opinion. On the contrary, we shall bear witness to our solidarity with the suffering brothers in a helpful manner only when we have the courage to express a critical solidarity. Precisely because Moses, the Prophets, the Psalms, and the Jew Jesus link us inseparably with Israel, its election, history, and mission, we must remind the Israelis (a) that the Bible does not speak of an ownership of soil and land but of a stewardship of God's property (e.g., Lev. 25:23); (b) that in the land which God has promised the stranger born in the land shall stand under the same law as the Jew (Exod. 12:49; Lev. 24:22; Num. 9:14; 15:15–16) and (c) that righteousness and mercy are not possible tasks *after* the battle for survival but are the prerequisites for life itself (Deut. 30:16; Lev. 18:5).

Finally we must, of course, be aware that for Jews the *land* of Israel and life in this land are matters of faith. We shall, however, not attempt to develop a New Testament "Theology of the Land." Rather, we shall continue to hold that after Auschwitz, the Jews have a rational and moral right to a state of their own, in which they cannot only defend themselves but also live in the way they choose. We know, however, that the Jews, ever since the days of their exile in the sixth century B.C., have for the most part lived without the benefit and the burden of a "Jewish state" and that they were preserved as a people with their own faith, in spite of all faint-heartedness and apostasy in their own ranks, even during frightful pogroms. Whereas the present State of Israel may be justified rationally, one cannot find in either the Old or the New Testaments any indication that a member of the Jewish people can only be a real Jew in a Jewish state. American Jews, too, are real Jews.

In the biblical summaries of the mighty acts of God as well as in the historical accounts on the various phases of Israel's history, mention is first made of the election and destination of the people, then of the promise and gift of the land, and only lastly of the formation of a state (in the forms of a tribal confederacy, a monarchy, or a priestly rule under foreign overloads). Two features distinguish the biblical picture of Israel's national history from the ideologies and historiography of other nations: (1) As Martin Buber has shown, the election, covenant, law, judgment, and grace of the One God are constitutive for the people, its land, and its state. Israel is destined to be unlike other nations, to administer the land as a steward in God's service, and to be ruled by a person or persons whose justice reflects God's own righteousness. Recent studies on the Law in the Old Testament have pointed out that no king in Israel is depicted as a creator of law: he and the people are to follow and to rediscover God's law. (2) In the Talmud and in Jewish liturgies God's vocation appears to establish a priority and preeminence of the people over the land, and of the land over the statehood; the people are called to obedience, faith, and hope even in the dispersion. The conviction of a final return to and gathering in the land is in most cases expressed without a reference to David (that is, to national Jewish sovereignty). Thus a simple equation of the essence and rank of people, land,

and state contradicts the biblical testimony as well as an important strand of Jewish self-understanding.

Can or must Christians give unconditional approval and
support to the present State of Israel? While consent to all
political decisions of the Ben Gurion, Meir, Rabin, and Begin
governments cannot be expected, we believe that the Jew Jesus
Christ and the solidarity of all members of the one (Old and
New Testament) people of God call upon all Christians and all
people of good will to give unconditional support to the Jewish
people, both in its dispersion and in the State of Israel. Israel's
election and mission, bound up by God with the promise of the
land, with the prescription of a righteous and merciful administration thereof, and with the permission to form a state, are the
basis for this approval, as the Dutch church document of 1971,
"Israel, People, Land and State" has indicated. The assertion
of the Israeli *State's* right to exist is, therefore, far from unconditional: it is qualified by the vocation of Israel to grant equal
rights (in biblical terms: to acknowledge the validity of "one
law") to the Jews *and* to the other inhabitants of the land.

Many Jews do not like to be reminded by third persons of
the Bible, of their mission, and of the serious temptation and
threat in which they find themselves. They point out that Western Christians are not involved in a fight for their very lives,
that our blatant co-responsibility for Auschwitz should prevent
us from bothering them with moralistic and political advice,
that we ourselves in our own states do not at all fulfill what we
are now demanding of them, that they have enough prophetic
voices in their own ranks, and that there will be sufficient time
for the establishment of righteousness after the political battle
for existence has ended in victory. Some of these reasons are
cogent; they almost have the effect of a club or a muzzle. And
yet they do not relieve us of the responsibility to speak, in full
knowledge of our own paramount guilt or complicity, especially
to our Jewish brothers, about God's promise and commandment.

The same applies also to our behavior towards Arab and
Palestinian Moslems, Christians, and atheists. It was and remains wrong for Western Christians to have been more con-

cerned about the Christian holy places in the Holy Land than about the life and future of Palestinian and Jewish men, women, and children—as expressed in the various proposals for the internationalization of Jerusalem. But this does not mean that we should remain silent about our disappointment over the behavior of such Christians who speak on behalf of a blind anti-Judaism and Arab nationalism or who are interested only in the security of their ecclesiastical properties. We refuse to join the chorus of those singing songs of hate against Israel or against the "Arabs." Pressures from either side, as exerted for instance by the denunciation of the World Council of Churches and individual Western Christians or by the threat to close the oil taps or revive worldwide Palestinian terrorist acts, should be called by their proper names: blackmail, and answered with the blunt refusal to yield.

We have already mentioned the divinely established peace mission of the people chosen by God. The road connecting West and East shall run through Israel. The blessing which it receives from God shall benefit all nations (Isa. 19:23–25; Gen. 12:1–3). Israel pays for its election by being tempted and chastised, as God's beloved child, in an especially hard way. Israel remains a thorn of God in the flesh of humankind and in the life of all nations, in order that God may not be forgotten. But Ishmael, too, the firstborn son of Abraham, whom the Koran calls the ancestor of the Arabs, stands under God's protection —and under his commandment (Gen. 16:10; 17:20; 21:18–20).

A church which for tactical reasons remains silent about this would be unfaithful to God and discredited before humankind. A church, however, which on every occasion speaks against sin, without making known the glad tidings entrusted to it, disavows its very self and makes itself superfluous. Those Christians who do not surrender the hope for reconciliation and, within the limits of their capabilities, for example, by working in a kibbutz or a Palestinian orphanage, bear witness to our solidarity with all suffering and hoping people, are doing something of what is necessary. They demonstrate that today's political situation is not simply forsaken by God. Belief in God and service to peace are not only inseparable but identical.